21st Century Essays
David Lazar and Patrick Madden, Series Editors

## Also by Phillip Lopate

*To Show and to Tell: The Craft of Literary Nonfiction*

*Portrait Inside My Head*

*At the End of the Day: Selected Poems*

*Notes on Sontag*

*Two Marriages*

*Waterfront*

*Getting Personal: The Selected Writings of Phillip Lopate*

*Totally, Tenderly, Tragically*

*Portrait of My Body*

*Against Joie de Vivre*

*The Rug Merchant*

*Bachelorhood: Tales of the Metropolis*

*Confessions of Summer*

*The Daily Round*

*Being With Children*

*The Eyes Don't Always Want to Stay Open*

Published by Mad River Books, an imprint of The Ohio State University Press.

Library of Congress Cataloging-in-Publication Data
Names: Lopate, Phillip, 1943– author, interviewer. | Lopate, Frances, 1918–2000, interviewee.
Title: A mother's tale / Phillip Lopate.
Other titles: 21st century essays.
Description: Columbus : Mad River Books, an imprint of The Ohio State University Press, [2017] | Series: 21st century essays
Identifiers: LCCN 2016037815 | ISBN 9780814213315 (cloth ; alk. paper) | ISBN 0814213316 (cloth ; alk. paper)
Subjects: LCSH: Lopate, Phillip, 1943—Family. | Lopate, Frances, 1918–2000—Interviews. | Entertainers—Biography. | Entertainers—Interviews. | Mothers and sons.
Classification: LCC PS3562.O66 Z46 2017 | DDC 818/.5403 [B]—dc23
LC record available at https://lccn.loc.gov/2016037815

Cover design by Christian Fuenfhausen
Text design by Juliet Williams
Type set in Adobe Sabon

∞ The paper used in this publication meets the minimum requirements of the American National Standard for Information Sciences—Permanence of Paper for Printed Library Materials. ANSI Z39.48–1992.

9 8 7 6 5 4 3 2 1

# A Mother's Tale

*Phillip Lopate*



Mad River Books, an imprint of
The Ohio State University Press / Columbus

# *Prologue*

When I was about eight years old, not long after I had mastered speech and a semblance of rationality, I became, or rather, fashioned myself into becoming, an ideal interlocutor for my mother. She would come to me with her troubles (usually complaints about my father), and I would listen with an expression of sympathy and knowingness, which I had learned to sham at an early age. What she was telling me was not so hard to grasp, even for an eight- or nine-year-old: she was unhappy, dissatisfied with my father and our shabby living circumstances, and had dreams of a finer existence, which included romantic love and a singing career. I nodded along, made the appropriate sounds of sympathy, and she would say something like "I can't believe I'm talking to a child, you're so grown-up, so understanding." I was pleased; that was my reward.

Years later, I came to resent what appeared to me an inappropriate seduction: she was unburdening herself at the same time as burdening me with adult problems, such as her sexual incompatibility with my father, that were robbing me of my innocence. Still years after that, when I came to question the very notion of childhood innocence, I realized that it had been a mutual seduction: I was every bit as complicit in offering myself as her confidant as she was in taking advantage of my offer. I loved my mother, and so what better way to ensure her attachment to me than by enacting a semblance of empathy?

This happy arrangement lasted until I was about fourteen, when I began to question her accounts or at least her interpretations of them. It seemed to me that she was being unjust in her assessment of my father, who was not nearly as blameworthy as she asserted, and I began to shift my sympathy from her to him (an unsurprising development in the individuation stage for an adolescent boy). Her long-held grudges also began to seem distorted. I started to chafe under her diva-like role in our family: her life story dominated, while the rest of us seemed reduced to minor characters orbiting around her. Granted, it was a compelling tale, but I was beginning to assert my own narrative, however pallid by comparison.

I now see that large parts of my adult personality and professional demeanor were formed in reaction to my mother: habits of detachment, skepticism, and thinking against oneself, which are classic essayist's equipment; resistance to melodrama; and a refusal to submit fully to empathy, as if it would involve signing onto, surrendering in a kind of trance to, another person's distortions and self-delusions. At the same time, I inherited from her a zest for storytelling, a passion for self-expression, and, I hope, some of her humor and psychological astuteness. We would always have much in common. But I could no longer be her "boy."

Though Frances Lopate could wax mawkish about her younger self, she also had the opposite tendency, a tart distaste for sentimentality. She would ridicule anything that seemed to her too soft or corny—a TV show, a song on the radio—dismissing it with acerbic sarcasm. Attracting any number of weaker souls in our working-class neighborhood, who would confide their troubles to her, she was happy to play the role of compassionate listener and amateur shrink. Sometimes, when one of these confidantes left our house tearfully after a soul-bearing session, my mother would tsk-tsk and say something like "Poor kid, she's got it bad." At other times, she would switch into her harsh-realism mode: "What an idiot! That doctor is never going to leave his wife for her." She had no sympathy for doormats.

I could never quite figure out which side of her would manifest in any given situation, or how the two opposing inner tendencies, sentimentality and scorn, got on with each other. When she was taking voice lessons, she would often practice a repertoire of torch songs of the Helen Morgan/Jane Froman variety, filled with longing and regret: "The Man I Love," "He's Just My Bill," "I Want a Sunday Kind of

Love," and "I Must Try to Make the Man Love Me." Her contralto voice was perfectly suited to those wonderfully schmaltzy tearjerkers. But she was quick to pounce on anyone else's self-pity or unrealistic fantasies.

My mother was psychologically minded—intrigued by hidden motives, contradictions, and paradoxes. Years later, when she went on the attack, taking offense at what she regarded as my insufficient love, I could always slow her down by interpreting her mixed messages. A narcissist, she appreciated whenever careful attention was paid to her, even if it came in the form of critical analysis.

I was thankfully spared that cliché of the overprotective Jewish mother, mine being far too self-absorbed to watch my every move. From age fifty on, she had a career in show business; but even before she began performing in dinner theater and doing commercials, she had that larger-than-life, self-dramatizing quality, like the actress-mother Madame Arkadina in Chekhov's *The Seagull.* Not that I was ever a suffering Konstantin, perishing under her neglect; I had enough conceit of my own to offset hers. Still, a part of me must have resented her egotism, because when I was in my forties I stupidly gave her a copy of Alice Miller's *The Drama of the Gifted Child,* a book then in vogue that blamed narcissistic mothers for their unhappy, overachieving children. She read it and said: "What are you trying to tell me? That it's all Mom's fault?" She was no dummy.

In 1984 I tape-recorded my mother telling her life story for a little over twenty hours. She would come downtown to the spacious loft I was subletting from a poet-friend in Tribeca, week after week, over the space of three summer months. (At the time, I was teaching in the University of Houston but would come back to New York City every chance I got.) My mother was a willing talker, never at a loss for words, and she had enough forthright candor and courage equal to the challenge. She was sixty-six at the time; I was forty-one. I suspect she had been waiting for her close-up all her life, and so this oral autobiography became, in a sense, the fantasized full-length interview. She may have also cooperated because it was a way to hang out with me, her younger son, for much longer periods of time than I was accustomed to doling out to her. While I thought about my mother constantly, she looming large in my imagination, the truth was that I preferred to reflect on her in private than spend actual "face-time" with her, guarded as I was for reasons both justifiable and inordinately self-protective.

She embraced the project wholeheartedly, though halfway through, she became wary about certain areas of interrogation, and suspicious of my possibly using the material as fodder for further writing. My previous efforts to portray her in print had left her bruised. By allowing herself to be tape-recorded, she may have envisioned finally setting the record straight and correcting whatever negative judgments I had had of her, once I understood where she was coming from. By the fifth taping session, she realized that I was still withholding the level of empathy she had hoped for, and began to accuse me of being "clinical." I, for my part, often wondered why I could *not* be more generously sympathetic to her tales of suffering—why they so often provoked impatience in me—when I tend to receive confessions of discontent from my students, my friends, and others (not excluding literary characters) with greater warmth.

To set the scene further, at the time of the taping my mother had four grown children: my older brother Leonard, who was already a popular radio interview host; myself, a writer-professor; and my younger sisters Betty Ann, a nurse-masseuse, and Joan, on her way to becoming a high-school English teacher. My mother had finally gotten her wish and divorced my father, but he was still living with her, due to her sense of obligation, perhaps, and the exigencies of New York real estate.

My mother died in 2000 at the age of 82. What strikes me as remarkable is that in the thirty-plus years that followed my 1984 recording of her, I never once listened to these tapes. They sat in a shoebox in the closet. Far from exploiting them for literary purposes—she was right in the end that I would, though it took me three decades to do so—I didn't even go near them. I think I was afraid of being overwhelmed by her intensity and also being made to feel how much I missed her. And in fact, it was unnerving when I finally transcribed them recently, her ghost voice filling my writing room. It was equally disconcerting to hear so many revelations that I had allowed myself to forget and to be put in contact with my younger self, the forty-one-year-old I once was. So I entered into a triangular dialogue involving my mother, my younger self, and the person I am today.

Listening to my mother's tapes impressed on me how often even an intelligent person can fail to observe the truth about herself. (That goes for almost everyone: I have a far easier time seeing other people's self-deceptions than my own.) Another curiosity was how someone goes about fashioning a life story from certain favorite anecdotes. Why those dozen and not a hundred others that might have proven equally significant? I am tempted to say that the signature of one's personality resides in just which recollected vignettes one chooses to keep retelling.

# A Mother's Tale

FRAN LOPATE

Just to make sure you don't forget me. Mommy

## *My Mother's Key Memory*

She would often relate an incident from her childhood. She was about nine. Her father lay dying in his bedroom. "It was four o'clock in the morning, and they pulled me out of bed. My feet were ice-cold without stockings, it was October, and it was so cold. And there I was standing at the head of the bed, because they were all lined up by age, all eleven of us, from the youngest, me, to the oldest, Mary. My mother was at the foot of the bed, crying. And my father was lying there. He looked all around, from one to the other, and he looked at me and he smiled at me. And Mary, from a great distance, said: 'Call him back, *Frumele*. Call him back! He'll come back for you.' There I was, with everybody's eyes on me. I couldn't speak. I couldn't speak. I had stage fright. Of course I couldn't call him back and make him live, the guy was dying! I tried. I called, 'Pop, Papa, Papa?' And he smiled at me. He rattled in his throat. He closed his eyes and he died. I couldn't call him back. And you know how many years that cost me on the couch, to get over the guilt that I couldn't call him back? You know how long it took me to get up on the stage, because of that? You know how many years I wasted not going into show business because of that?"

"But you were only nine years old. You must have known you didn't have that power."

"I didn't know. I didn't know anything. I had an empty head. I couldn't reason. I wasn't sure if I was sleeping or awake. I just knew that I was *embarrassed*. And all those years later, I thought: I'm guilty, I killed my father, because when I had the chance to call him back, I didn't. All I could do was say in a weak voice, 'Papa?' I should have gone all out, I should have really CALLED him. But it stuck in my throat: what came out was a little nothing. And it was my fault. All those years, an audience terrified me, because every time I got up in front of an audience, I was right back there at my father's bedside. And nobody could understand it, I could never describe it, because I could never tell anybody what the problem was. I was ashamed. I couldn't even tell my shrink. It was only when I could explain it to him that I realized that's what the problem was, and I was able to go out there and face an audience. And now I know my papa had forgiven me because my papa had been protecting me. I say, 'Thank you, Papa, because if I had called you back it only would have been more agony for you, more pain.' I wouldn't wish that kind of pain on anyone. Certainly not on one whom I loved. I still feel my father around me. When I go to Reverend Craig [a spiritualist my mother consulted], he is always looking over my shoulder and seeing him. If it hadn't been for my father, I would have been killed in Jerusalem. I sincerely believe it."

My mother offered this anecdote as the historical hinge, the source of all the anguish and injustice she had suffered and would continue to suffer. "How can you tell a—a little kid to do such a thing?" she sputtered. "How can you be so heartless as to put a child through that?"

Above and beyond my skepticism about her father's ghost intervening to protect her, I was always suspicious of my mother's tendency to sensationalize her pain, which I equated with insincerity. I had no doubt the incident had scarred her; but I saw it differently. First, it was self-evident she couldn't have done anything to revive her father, so why the lingering guilt? (I understand, such feelings are not rational, but one might hope the conscious, rational mind might eventually weigh in and temper their power.) Second, why hold it against her siblings for life, when they may very well have been desperate too at that moment, and, acting out of desperation, hoped for a miracle. There *are,* after all, recorded accounts of a loved one's voice calling someone back from the brink of mortality. Granted, maybe they were wrong to have put her on the spot that way, but what made their request so outrageous as to be unforgiveable for life?

I suspect the real wound, the real abandonment, was her father's dying, not her being unable to save him. But that possibility could never be acknowledged. Her loss was immediately displaced onto resentment at her siblings and shame at being asked to perform a deed she was powerless to do.

My mother's unlocking of this memory as the key to performing onstage speaks to a particular postwar version of watered-down Freudianism. Hollywood plots like *Spellbound* turned on bringing to the surface some repressed memory, which would then liberate the character from his or her fears. While I continue to subscribe to the value of Freud and psychotherapy, this "trick" of unlatching the unconscious with a single buried recollection has come to seem—not just to me, but to the culture at large—simplistic and overly optimistic. Would that the human psyche could be disentangled so neatly! While my mother believed that her ability to embark on a show business career occurred precisely because she was able to cough up this tidbit to her shrink, I think it had more to do with her finally having cleared the interior space and acquired enough technical skill as a singer and performer to engage in those pursuits.

## *Her Papa*

My mother's father came from a long line of people characterized by her as "the intelligentsia." In her telling: "His father was a cantor in a big temple. My father sang, but he knew that if he stayed in that temple, he would not be able to earn a living as a cantor. He graduated from the University of Leipzig, and lived in Leipzig and Dresden, and started to make a reputation for himself as a designer. He loved fur, and he became a couturier, a very famous designer of furs. But at that time there were rumblings in Europe of anti-Semitism, so he wanted to come to America. His name had a 'von' in it, left over from an ancestor's relationship with one of the Emperor's relatives, who had married this Jew. They even gave him a title, I believe it was Baron von Berlow. But there was too much resentment from the nobility, so he dropped the 'von.' When he came to

New York, in order to attract a classy clientele, he took up the 'von' again."

These aristocratic pretensions inspired mockery and mirth when we were growing up in the slums of Brooklyn. My mother would boast that her father's family was "related to the Kaiser," and we would respond: "How could he be related to the Kaiser when we were Jewish?" She stuck to her story: it could have been true, who knows? Though she sometimes said her father was Polish, there was undoubtedly snobbism in her family's identification as German. Later, when she married my father, Albert, who came from Russian Jewish stock, she regarded him in the superior way German Jews did Eastern European Jews, as *Ostjuden,* semibarbarians, uncultured and unwashed. I am therefore the product of the most fraught of mixed marriages: German Jew and Russian Jew. The irony is that when my brother Leonard found my mother's birth certificate after her death, it stated that her parents' country of origin was the Ukraine, which would have made her every bit as *Ostjude* as Father. But to continue her account:

"My father stayed in New York for a very short time. The first thing that happened when he came to New York, this had to be 1893 or 1894, he looked up his sister, who had married a man named Herman Guerseney. Herman had a younger sister about sixteen years old who happened to be my mother, and my father sent for her to arrange a marriage, although he was considerably older than she was, about fourteen years older, and considerably shorter. All of her brothers were enormous men: they had to duck when they went through a doorway. And my father was shorter. But not so much weaker, or else he couldn't have knocked out all those children.

"My mother was getting ready to marry him, but she did not like New York. She was used to more gracious living. For one thing, the Jews that came over congregated on the Lower East Side, and she wouldn't tolerate that. She couldn't stand the dirt, she couldn't stand the noise. My mother was a very elegant lady. And she said 'I won't live like this. Either you take me out of here, or we won't get married.' At that time Herman and his wife, my father's sister

Anna, decided to move to Boston, which was considered an elegant city, with lots of wealthy people who could use the services of my father."

My mother's family also had a brother named Marcus, who had moved to Boston. This Marcus, my mom used to tell us, had invented the cylinder phonograph, but he didn't have capital to manufacture it, so he sold the patent to another inventor—this nefarious guy named Thomas Alva Edison—for a pittance, and Edison made millions off it, taking all the credit. A dubious family myth: it is commonplace for immigrant families to claim an Uncle Marcus, an unsung genius robbed of the profits of his brilliance by his lack of Yankee ruthlessness. "Marcus never had enough know-how to go after the people who had the patents. All he had was a collection of wives and children. The wives he never bothered to divorce—somehow he managed to get married again. Marcus was the one who died sitting up. His daughter-in-law got so scared when she saw him sitting up with the spoon in his hand and a boiled egg still in his spoon that she ran out of the room. Before the family could do anything about it, rigor mortis had set in. And they couldn't lay him down to get him in the coffin" [my mother laughs boisterously at this point in the tape] "so they had to saw him in half. One of his sons remarked that they should bury him twelve feet deep instead of six feet to make sure he wouldn't get up, and drive a stake through his heart."

"Why?"

"Why? Because he did whatever he wanted to do, with complete disregard for anybody else's welfare but his own. He never supported his kids; he never paid any attention to them. And they hated him for that. He died a month after my father died. I didn't really know the man. But I do remember, when he came to visit my father, he was dressed in an overcoat with a velvet collar, a derby hat and spats. Whatever he wore was of the highest quality, and his wife and children would go around in rags.

"In America my father still considered himself a cousin of the Kaiser. During the First World War, before I was born, he was very pro-Germany. He was lucky that he didn't land in jail. He used to be the official designer for the Massachusetts State functions; he would make the ladies' ball gowns. He was big stuff. But as soon as he started sounding off about 'my cousin the Kaiser,' forget it! They threw him out of the Massachusetts State Building, where he had his office. He lost his business; he lost everything he had, because he was so pro-German. He was out on his ass. That was when I was born, in 1918, when everything started to fall apart. He had to work piecemeal from then on.

"After he became sick he would get up the energy to climb to the attic, where he had his workroom, his tables all spread out. To his dying day he used to take little jobs, subcontracting from clothing stores to make coats. When he went off to work, before he was too sick to leave the house, he'd come home always with something in his pocket. Even if it was just an orange, it had to be divided in three parts, for the three youngest children, Dorothy, Gladys, and me. He was kindly toward the others; the difference was, I got the extra hug. You have no idea the envy that used to emanate from them. He was very affectionate to me. He would hold me on his lap between his knees and stroke my hair. I had golden curls. My parents doted on me, and I knew it. He would tell me how special I was; he said I had a golden voice, and my sister Larly was telling me I was shit. I didn't know who to believe. I grew up confused."

Grateful as I must have been for this detailed family lore, and finding it interesting up to a point, I suspect I was also a little bored or unable to connect with it, as I still am. In general, ancestral history always seems to me a story full of holes, and what remains, largely self-serving. In this case, my mother was preparing the ground for her Joseph role, as the favorite child who would be set upon by her siblings. There was no getting around it: I was in for a dose of her self-pity.

"My father could never raise his voice. My mother was the one who had to yell at us. My memories of him growing up were that he was always sick. He got that waxy yellow look. He always listened to music. He would put the German paper down and tell my sisters to start practicing. Dorothy would play the violin and Gladys would accompany her on the piano, and he would listen while reading the paper. If she hit a sour note he would look up from the paper and say '*Fauss!*' and go back to his paper.

"His sister, Aunt Anna, would sometimes stop by. She was what you call a black witch. You know the pictures of the Italian women with mustaches? That's what Anna looked like. She was jealous of my mother. She used to accuse my mother of wishing my father dead, because my mother looked so good in black. When Aunt Anna came to visit she would bring a cloud to the house. Anna would cry, 'My baby brother, my baby brother!' as though we were murdering him. My God, the man was dying from Hodgkin's disease, pernicious anemia, silicosis, and every horrible ill you can think of. My mother had nothing to do with it; she wanted to keep him alive. I can't imagine why—the man was so sick. It was merciful that he died when he did."

## *Her Mother*

"My mother's parents were well-to-do businesspeople in Riga. Riga at the time was ruled by Germany, so they considered themselves German. My mother was involved with a young man whom her parents didn't approve of, a peasant boy, so they shipped her off to America to marry a man they did approve of, my father.

"My mother was a hardworking woman. But once a week, no matter if the laundry was piled up, if the diapers were full or piss was running on the floor, my mother would get dressed in her finest clothes, which my father had made for her, and go to the theater. She used to say, 'I am also a child. I'm my mother's child. I'm entitled to one day a week.' She was an attractive woman, and she had plenty of opportunities to walk away from that scene of one kid after the other. She didn't have to stay. There was one actor who used to chase her for years. His name was Donald Meek."

Donald Meek was a character actor, slight and balding, who appeared in dozens of Hollywood movies, including ones by classy directors such as John Ford, Fritz Lang, Tay Garnett, and George Cukor. Just as my mother rued rejecting the guys who'd pursued her when she was younger and whom she could have married, who went on to become big successes, so she fantasized about the ones her mother had let get away.

"My mother was a snob, I guess. One of the first things she did when she came to America was go to school. She didn't believe in hanging onto her accent. She had a faint German accent, which was charming, but she spoke in English. She enjoyed English theater and English movies. She didn't read English too well. My sister Dorothy would get books out of the library and read to her while she was ironing or baking. She didn't like gushy stuff; she liked a good mystery. My mother wasn't stupid; she had to be intelligent and strong because she was a Scorpio. But she just had too many children."

[I too am a Scorpio. Perhaps my mother was alluding to that fact as an indirect compliment. Then again, she knew that I have absolutely no belief in astrology.]

"According to my sisters, my mother's philosophy was: 'When you marry, you should be the more attractive and the smarter, because that way you'll always have it over him. He'll never be able to leave you for someone else because he'll never find anyone better than you.' She was more attractive than my father, oh yes." [This bit of wisdom my mother obviously took to heart, with mixed results.]

"After my father died, my mother had a number of suitors. She was all set to marry again. The men were lined all the way up the block. There were a couple of romances my mother had that year. I remember her going in a car with one guy, she found out he was married. . . . The druggist on the block, Kolodny, he was tall, thin, a nice guy, he was always bringing her a box of candy, and I think he was the one she had finally settled on. Everyone that came in to court my mother, my sister Larly would make fun of. This one was too short, that one too fat. This one was bald, that one had too much hair. This one was not rich enough, that one was too rich. If one was musical and played a clarinet, she would make fun of his clarinet. Whatever it was, it made no difference, she would ridicule. My sister Larly—I don't think the word 'bitch' is strong enough. There's no describing the cruelty of that woman. My mother was ready to tell her to go fuck herself. She knew she needed an operation, she had these fibroid tumors. She figured, 'I'll have the operation, I'll take my youngest daughters, I'm getting the hell away from Larly.' She was 48, 49 when she died. My mother went to the hospital for an operation that was relatively simple, a hysterectomy, and the operation was a success. The only problem was, peritonitis set in. We went to visit her in the hospital, Larly and I. She was not well. By the time we got home on the trolley, there was a phone call: Come back to the hospital, your mother has passed away."

## *In Her Sister's Care*

Frances, as she said, was the youngest of eleven children. "There was Mary, Charlie, Maxie, Larly, Uddie, Lily, Sarah, George, Dorothy, Gladys, and me. My sister Uddie—her real name was Rose—died right after my father died. Uddie was twenty-two years old when she died. My father died in October 1927. My sister Uddie lived until January 1928. She was a lyric soprano: she was all set to make her debut on the concert stage. Her concert tour was to start in Miami, in this big concert hall they had just built, and a week or so before, she tragically had a heart attack. Today, with the new open heart surgery, she would have lived. She had such dark eyes that even when her lids were closed in the coffin, it seemed like she was looking at us. I was a little kid, I was scared. Then my mother lasted another year, and she died, too. One right after the other.

"My older siblings were a generation older, and we had very little in common. There was only one person in the family who had any real affection for me, and that was Max. I don't think he had a devious bone in his body. When my parents died, he said, 'Come to me, I'll take you.' And Larly said: 'No! We cannot separate the three girls.' Larly insisted that my mother had said to her: 'Take care of the three girls, make ladies out of them.' Shit, she couldn't make a lady out of her own daughter! Larly was about twenty-six at that time. Her real name was Ruth: her birth certificate said Rochelle, but she was called Larly and I don't know why. Dorothy was already working part-time. Gladys was in high school. So she took us in. But there was no love involved. A child knows when it's loved. A child sure knows when it's not loved."

My mother had needed a mother and she got her older sister Larly, who was hoping to start her own family and found herself burdened with this morose, grieving, sassy eleven-year-old. (Disloyally, I can also see my aunt's point of view.) At thirteen, my mother had had enough, and ran away from home. That's another story, which we will get to soon enough. For the moment, let's pause and consider the narratives we make of our lives, and which events we choose to obsess over.

"Release from the wounds of childhood is a task never completed, not even on the point of death," writes Vivian Gornick. Whether this is invariably true, it appears to have been the case with my mother. At my Aunt Mary's burial, I witnessed my mother, by then close to seventy, take a shovel of dirt and fling it on the coffin, muttering under her breath, but loud enough to be heard by the other mourners, "There! That should keep the old witch!" I was appalled at her evergreen vindictiveness, after six decades, yet I admired the fresh stores of vitality her anger always provided her.

Back to my mother. "I loved my father, because he was so giving, so warm. My mother was also the kind who could take me on her lap. They were both very affectionate people, and I was always the recipient of that affection. To have both go at a time that was so crucial for a child, and then to be thrown to the 'tender mercies' of my sister, who didn't give a shit whether I lived or died. . . . After my father died, they didn't try to develop my music because there was no music in my house anymore. For three solid years that piano was closed. Nobody sang, nobody danced. My sister Larly used to make me wear black socks, with a black ribbon in my hair. Until my brother Charlie came and got so furious that he gave her hell for it, and made her take it off.

"I've been thinking a lot about Larly, and I think I figured out that her problem was sex. When boys played with me, she was always worried that something else was going to happen. She was right in the middle—the Edwardian Age was ending and the Flapper Age came along. It affected girls one way or the other: either they became flappers, cut their hair, smoked cigarettes, and wore their dresses up to their *pupiks,* or they became prudes. She became a prude, I think, because she was afraid of what she was feeling."

As I listen again to the tape I am processing a few items differently from my mother. First, the fact that nobody sang or danced for three years points to a depth of grief in which the whole family was plunged, not just my mother. She saw that pall as merely a pretext to deprive her of a chance to develop her musical talents. Second, my mother's assessment of her sister as a prude speaks to her staking a claim of her own as a sexual being, more honest and bohemian about acting on her desires than her bourgeois sister would ever be.

"Why do you think Larly wanted to take in the three girls?" I hear my younger interviewer-self ask on the tape.

"Well, she didn't like housework! She wanted three maids. She figured that she could stay in her room, and the dishes would be done and the lunch would be made and the house would be vacuumed." [Somehow I doubt that my mother's older sister took on the task of raising three orphaned girls solely because it provided her with free maid service, but we'll let it stand.] "Larly had a two-bedroom apartment in Jamaica, Queens, which meant that Gladys and Dorothy shared a bedroom, Larly and her husband Sam shared a bedroom, and there was no room for me. So I was given a day bed in the sunroom, which had windows all around, on three sides. And no curtains, which meant I had to go to bed after dark and get up before it was light. It was a very busy corner, 158th Street and Hillside Avenue. That was one of the more miserable times of my life. I had been taking French in the seventh grade in Boston. I was a bright kid. I had gotten all As and Bs, up to the seventh grade, despite the fact that the school would call and say Frances is not working hard. Today I would be called a gifted underachiever. After my mother died I was moved to Cedarhurst on Long Island. That was when everything started going downhill, right down the drain. They were all wealthy kids, and I was an outsider. For one thing they made fun of the way I spoke with a Boston accent. The teacher loved it, the kids hated it. I was starting to get a little bit chunky, and I had long sausage curls. My clothes were abysmal, because they would never spend money on me. I couldn't wear Gladys's hand-me-downs because she was so small. I was always wearing Mary's old shoes with the heels so worn down I was walking on the back of my stockings. Somehow or other, I didn't fit in. I never made friends. And I was very unhappy. Mary let her children stay home for every little fart, or if it was raining. But Larly would make me go to school if it was a shitstorm. I would walk to school and I would see Mary's kids playing on the sun porch, and they'd wave to me. And I would trudge on to school. Of course I was jealous; I wanted that kind of treatment. But I never got it. Wherever they needed a maid, they would send me. I didn't want to go to my brother George's house and pick up the shitty diapers of his little girl. She was a rotten baby. And their other boy was a dull, stupid child. I washed the floor, I scrubbed the clothes, I cleaned, I cooked, I took care of two kids, and I didn't want to be a fucking maid for them. So I kept running away."

It is somewhat difficult to square my mother's version of her older sisters as satanic with the memories I have of my aunts Gladys, Dorothy, and Larly, all of whom lived in Queens or Long Island, and whom we saw from time to time. They struck me as harmless, bland, conventionally complacent middle-class women. Gladys, the youngest and friendliest, had a chirpy manner, played piano at social events, and was married to Morris, an attorney, who had a bristly mustache, glasses, and a perpetual sneer, like Groucho Marx but without the mirth. Dorothy seemed reserved and was said to paint, awfully, in her spare time, and she was married to David, the crew-cut manager of a large stationery store in Manhattan. Larly, the dreaded Larly, was a cipher, or at least left no impression on me, and neither did her portly, bald husband Sam, who worked in insurance. All three sisters had latched onto "good providers," men unlike my father, and seemed to regard us warily, as though our bohemian penury might be catching. We in turn condescended to them as materialistic philistines who knew nothing about Art. On those occasions when all the clans got together, they seemed cautious around us, either out of an innate inexpressiveness or fear of my mother's tart tongue. Once, one of my aunts, on a rare visit to our modest quarters in Brooklyn, commented "Oh, a bathroom," and my mother, without missing a beat, said, "Yes, they're putting them in apartments these days." At these gatherings, my siblings and I behaved stiffly, barely concealing our boredom, while our aunts seemed baffled at our hauteur. Gladys might say with her parting hug, "Don't be a stranger!" and we might smile ironically, thinking that "stranger" was precisely what we were and always would be. Years later, my mother would relay gossip to us about her sister's children, our nieces and nephews, this one's divorce and that one's failed catering business, in contrast to, say, those world-renowned successes, Lenny and me.

## *The Runaway*

Growing up, I was fascinated with the story of my mother running away from home, and would try to get her to tell it in greater detail. She was always frugal with specifics. In interviewing her, I finally saw an opportunity to learn what happened. Here was her version, which she told with considerable hesitation.

"The first time I ran away for good, I was fifteen. I took whatever money I found lying around the house, from Dorothy's little *pushky* [piggy bank] and Gladys's little *pushky* and Larly's grocery money. I packed a suitcase and I went to a place called Bayonne, New Jersey. The reason I went to Bayonne was because that was the next bus that was leaving from the bus terminal. I didn't want to go home, but I was only fifteen years old. Some guy picked me up at a bus stop, and said he would take me to a place where I could get a job. And of course in the car he tried to rape me. When I put up a fight he opened the door and threw me out. Fortunately it was on a suburban street, not out in the woods, so I was able to pick myself and walk back to a bus stop. I asked someone at the bus stop where I could find a place to stay, and he told me to go to the Salvation Army.

"I was feeling that I didn't like men. That's when I started building defenses, brick walls around myself. Anyway, it was not a pleasant experience. I did manage to find a place to stay at the Salvation

Army shelter. But then some woman at the Salvation Army said: 'Hey, why don't you come with me, see if you can get a job waiting on tables in this bar.' So I went with her to the bar and started working there. But they didn't want a waitress, they wanted a hostess. What they really wanted was a pair of hookers. And this woman—was a hooker. So it was just another repetition of what had happened in the car. There was a guy who was a patron, a regular—men like to use their hands, and I'm not terribly into that. I was very young, and I really didn't know how to fend off this sort of thing. I couldn't laugh it off. To me there were only two ways of dealing with it: either give in, or escape. The most sensible way was to escape. I escaped, and I walked back to the Salvation Army. Now, where did I get my sense of morality? It had to be from my sister Larly, who was very moral, strict, very rigid. So for that I thank her. She really did save my life, by giving me that sense of morality. The problem after that was when I grew older, the sense of morality remained so rigid that it became a stumbling block, and even though I tried to live a different kind of life, it never really allowed me to enjoy anything I tried outside of the norm. Whatever the norm is."

Eventually, the reason for her hesitation in telling the runaway episode came out. Several tape sessions later, she admitted that she had lost her virginity during this time. I am putting the incident here in its chronological sequence, rather in the order of her telling:

"I had only slept with one guy, it was the breaking of the maidenhead. It happened when I ran away from home. It was practically rape. With his wife's blessings, strangely enough. I had a little furnished room in New Jersey. And this young couple had a furnished room in the house too, and I remember she said she had her period, and he was horny as hell. She said, 'Go ahead, because if you don't, I'm going to have to do something myself.' She didn't want to. And he went ahead. I didn't even know who he was. I never saw him again. It was very strange, because it was something I did not enjoy, it was painful, it was unpleasant, it was rushed. And I said to myself, *That* was what my sister Larly was cautioning me against? She didn't have to worry about it ever again, because that was not interesting to me. It was not fun. I couldn't understand why these girls were doing it for fun, when it wasn't fun."

Listening to this account again, I am somehow not surprised: I had always suspected a sexual episode had occurred during the running away. I feel sorry for my mother, for having been taken advantage of in that manner. It had to have been gruesome. Still, I can't decide what to make of her saying that it was "practically rape," when she had clearly agreed to go along with the wife's request, as a favor to another put-upon woman. I can imagine her own sense of powerlessness, on the road, succumbing finally to outside pressure, which may have merged with a curiosity to experience this naughty act she had so been warned against.

It may strike the reader as unseemly for me to be ruminating here about my mother's first sexual experience. I'll only say in my defense that all my life my mother had a way of sexualizing every conversation. In telling her life story she was preoccupied with the thread of her own sexual awakening. When I was younger, my impulse was to change the subject; I became squeamish when she began talking about sex. Ultimately, I developed a thicker shell, and recognized that, in interviewing her about her history, I would have to take a neutral stance toward this material, which was obviously so crucial to her. She was both eager and loath to relate it to me.

"However, the Salvation Army got me a job as a mother's helper—a sleep-in maid. And unfortunately, I broke some sort of an antique vase. The people got very upset and hollered and screamed, and intimidated me to the point that I told them where I lived, where I came from, and they got in touch with my family. My family sent my brother Max to come and pick me up. He took me back to his house."

## *The Prodigal Daughter Returns*

There followed a period of domestic instability, her being shipped back and forth between Boston, Queens, and Long Island. Frances found that while she was gone, her sister Larly had moved to another, smaller apartment, and refused to take her back. Clearly

Larly had been appalled by her younger sister's running away, which she must have regarded as wanton and borderline-criminal. Larly said that if Frances balked at going to her sister Mary's, she would be sent to a home for delinquent minors who were runaways. "I think I'd have been better off if they'd put me in an orphanage after my parents died. I would have at least had a sense of belonging, even if it was just to an orphanage. This way I had no roots, I had no family, no nothing." [Not quite true: but there was no point in my challenging every dramatic heightening or exaggeration in my mother's storytelling.]

From Mary's house she was shunted off to her brothers Max and George. Eventually she took a place of her own, a furnished room. By this time she was sixteen, a high school dropout who was finally able to get working papers and would gladly accept any kind of work. A friendly Polish woman named Catherine suggested she work at the Automat (a storied proto-fast-food institution: dishes were placed behind windows; the patrons fed the appropriate number of coins into a slot and pulled out the desired dish), picking up dirty dishes from the tables. But Larly nixed the idea, saying, "No sister of mine is going to be a waitress, with men putting their hands all over her." Catherine tried to argue that such things didn't happen in the Automat. "People go in there to eat and leave." Larly refused to let her waitress, and was equally adamant that she not be allowed to go on relief. The Depression having spawned the New Deal, Frances fantasized getting into one of the WPA's musical or acting programs; but again, no dice. "God knows what I could have done, if she hadn't stood in my way of becoming a human being."

In social class terms, she was in a bind: Her lineage may have been middle class, but her new, downwardly mobile reality put her in the working class. Being the black sheep of a respectable middle-class family meant she was still expected to uphold its standards of propriety: hence, no going on welfare, working as a waitress, or accepting WPA-sponsored employment. All the more credit must be given to her resilience.

"Anyway, I took a little job here and a little job there. I worked in a factory, making cards for signs. I worked in a department store during the Christmas rush. I managed to survive. When I didn't have my rent money, I managed to get that from my sister Larly."

It isn't clear to me why, if she was living by herself at this point, she needed to submit to the dictates of her sister. Perhaps it's because, as she briefly admitted, she was taking money from Larly to pay her rent. Beyond that, she seemed to regard Larly as a surrogate mother, whose authority she honored, however reluctantly, and whose disapproval she nurtured with assiduous bitterness all the days of her life.

A key anecdote in the chain of wrongs done her was the Big Storm. Let her tell it. "In 1938 there was a hurricane in New York, and Larly insisted I go to temple. So I did. I went back to her house for dinner. She wouldn't let me stay overnight, or until the hurricane died down. She insisted that I leave. I went out, and the water was up to my knees. I got on the trolley, I went back to my room, I was shivering. One of the men who had a room on the same floor took my coat off and hung it up, took my shoes off, took my stockings off, sat me on a chair and poured me a cup of cocoa, rubbed my hands and rubbed my feet, he wrapped my feet up in towels, until I stopped shaking. Then he took me by the hand and led me back into my room. People were kind to me. There *are* kind people in the world. They just don't happen to be in my family."

Frances was already twenty years old at the time. It's surprising that such a headstrong young woman as my mother would submit to the injunction that she attend synagogue in the middle of a hurricane.

"How Jewish was your family when you were growing up?" I asked.

"Not much. We didn't go to Sabbath services. My father belonged to an Orthodox temple, but he didn't go every Saturday because there were many times he had to work. He went only on high holidays. My mother kept a kosher house, but she didn't get panicky if a spoon that had been used for ice cream got mixed in with a meat dish. With a whole bunch of children doing dishes, you can't always keep track. The Passover Seders I do remember. But we didn't throw out all the *chometz* [food that was not expressly made for Passover] because we didn't have enough money to: she would store the cereal or the crackers in a box in the hallway, until after Pesach was over, then bring it out again. We had enormous Seders. The dining room table was round, and three or four leaves we would put in so that it made an enormous oval. Added to that were some kind of folding tables. We didn't have enough chairs for all the children, so they would take two chairs and put a board across it, and we would sit on the board. My father would go through the whole Seder service, because he was a singer. He would sing and sing in Hebrew, with his glasses on the end of his nose, and explain to us what he was singing. He also sang the Christmas carols in German in the Hollverein Society. He was an assimilated Jew. Like me. The ceremonies, the rites, the traditions were important. Not the actual religion.

"I have all sorts of dichotomous feelings about Judaism. I believed in God when I was growing up, as I do now. I'm a deist. I guess I had the same conception of God as a child that everyone else had—the man with the beard, the Michelangelo conception, because there was no other, until I started thinking for myself. Today I only pray for my children, I don't pray for things for myself. 'Don't bother with me, God, 'cuz I'm okay, I'll do all right by myself, but if You can possibly see the way clear, do something for the kids.' Once a week I buy a lotto ticket, I pick out my six numbers, and I say 'I would be satisfied with a half a million.' The first thing I'd do after Uncle Sam took his cut, I'd divide it into five equal portions: the four kids and me. I don't pray for your father. I just want him out of my life. That's all I would pray for, if I did pray about him. I don't wish for anyone's death. I don't want him to die, because if I had wanted him to die, I wouldn't have prayed so hard when he was in the hospital. I wanted him to live. I just didn't know what agony he was going to give me. But I couldn't pray for his death because it would be wrong. And I do believe in sin, or trying not to sin. I believe in retribution, one way or another. I don't label it karma, but it's still the same thing."

So be thankful for small favors: She did not actively pray for my father's death. She just wished he would disappear.

## *Boyfriends before Marriage*

"I was very leery of guys. I was always afraid that what they wanted was not friendship, not romance; they always wanted to get in. And if that's what they wanted, I didn't want it. I'd have a date or two, and as soon as a hand started moving around, that's when I cut and ran. I wasn't a beauty. I had a gorgeous figure. But don't forget I had that big nose and wore glasses. I was not a beautiful girl. I was homely. It was the body that turned everybody on. It was all sex appeal. And evidently, inadvertently, I used sex appeal as a way to attract them. But I attracted the wrong aspect of them, which I didn't want. Or maybe I did want that but didn't know I wanted it. Whatever it was, it was all very confusing. I was caught in the middle of something I didn't know anything about, it was too hard for me to handle."

She had one boyfriend she almost married, named Harry Rosen. He was rich, he was nice, he had put a deposit on a car, he gave her a beautiful engagement ring. "But he was boooring. I met Daddy and I sneaked out on a blind date. Daddy was not boring. In fact he was very interesting. Harry Rosen's brother found out. So without any big *tsimmes* I gave him back his ring, said 'Thank you very much.' And that was that."

When we were growing up, my mother would refer to various old beaux who had turned out to be big moneymakers. Unlike my father. The one she adverted to most was a fellow named Butch. He was the boyfriend of a girl with whose family my mother was living. The family looked down on Butch because he worked at a gas station; they said, "Butch will never amount to much." So the girl went off and married someone else. Butch went on to own several gas stations, he become very rich, while the guy his ex-girlfriend married ended up working in the post office, my mother recalled.

Butch was a live wire, a real go-getter. He liked to dance, though he was a terrible dancer, and my mother was such a good dancer that she was the only one who could keep up with him. "That's one of the things that I have not forgiven Daddy for," she notes parenthetically, "because he refused to learn to dance." Anyway, "Butch was a lot of fun. We were part of a whole crowd, all guys except for me, I was the only girl accepted into the group. They didn't like Butch's girlfriend because she nagged. She hated cigars, and she would say 'Bernie!' when he lit one up—his name was Bernie—and he would blow the smoke in her face. I also hated cigars, but I would ask him calmly to put it out and he would do it for me." [Why am I getting the feeling that this Butch, who cavalierly blew smoke in his girlfriend's face, would not have been my idea of fun?]

## *My Parents Meet on a Blind Date*

"Butch would close the gas station around eleven o'clock and I knew that about a quarter after eleven his Franklin, a big old boat of a car, would be there to pick me up. We would ride to Montauk Point just to take a ride. He never tried too hard to have sex, which I appreciated. The night that I met Daddy, Butch had blind-dated me with Daddy, because he wanted to get laid, and he took this other girl out. I got in the back seat with this tall guy with glasses, and Butch got in the front seat with this girl. I said, 'What in hell is going on here?' and he said, 'I'll tell you later.' We went to a diner and had something to eat. He took the girl home, and a half hour later he came back and said, 'Okay, we got that out of our system.' Then the three of us went back to that diner, which was one of our favorite hangouts. We talked and talked. We started out at eleven o'clock and we ended up at four, just talking. Butch was a great talker. Daddy was very quiet at first. He listened to Butch and me. Then he started talking, analyzing me. He said I was an introvert pretending to be an extrovert. He had me sized up right. I was very impressed. Throw psychological terms at me, I'm impressed. Albert Lopate always knew how to impress me. He knew that my strategy had been to never show how intelligent I was: that was the hook. The only thing he didn't know was that I was a brain-picker. I was going to pick his brain, and when there was nothing left, I was going to leave him. Only by the time I had his brain picked it was too late, I couldn't leave him! He talked literature to me. He would tell me stories from Schnitzler, Hermann Hesse. A lot of these things I couldn't read. Hermann Hesse I just couldn't absorb. I had a young thirsty mind, but it wasn't an analytical mind. And he had a good analytical mind, and he would digest it for me. I would sit there like at the Master's feet and listen to these stories. Then when it came to music, I would take him to concerts, because I was interested in music. He was bored out of his skull, but it didn't make any difference, I would take him anyway. That's when I discovered Lewisohn Stadium, where we sat on concrete benches. It was wonderful."

So many of these details—the Lewisohn Stadium concerts, the favorite diner, the pop psychology terms "introvert/extrovert"—seem redolent of that historic moment: listening to them, I am like the character in Delmore Schwartz's story "In Dreams Begin Responsibilities," who sees his parents' courtship on the movie screen. Knowing how sad their marriage will turn out, he wants to tell them Stop! But he's powerless to impede the family fate. Me, I'm the opposite: I am rooting for this tall proletarian guy with glasses who is reading Schnitzler on his own. I am thinking, Forget the cruder charms of that *putz* Butch, go with the guy with the analytical mind who reads. For my sake, and the sake of future generations.

## *Shame and Its Aftermath*

After my parents started dating, my mother took a beautician course and found steady work in a beauty parlor. Everything seemed to be going well until one day she ran into an old acquaintance from the neighborhood. He said, "Gee, I haven't seen you in years. Where have you been?" She said, "Out of town and back." He offered to buy her a cup of coffee. When they were sitting down in a coffee shop, he said, "Did you have the baby?" "What baby?!" she asked. It turned out her sister Larly had been telling people, including the police, during the period she ran away that they didn't know where she was and that she was pregnant. The police rounded up all the young men from the Jamaica Jewish Center and, one by one, interrogated them, accusing each of being the father. My mother had not known any of this, but she sensed she had a reputation for being loose and didn't know where it came from.

"All that time Daddy was trying to get into me, and I was not letting him. That's why he couldn't understand all this talk about me. When he took me to a basketball game, a guy went over to him and said, 'Oh, I see you're out with Frances. She really puts out, doesn't she?' Daddy says: 'Not to me. Did she do it with you?'—'No, not with me, but with *him.*' So Daddy went to *him.* And the guy says, 'Oh sure she puts out, but not with me, but with *him.*' So Daddy went to him. Every guy was pointing to every other guy, and nobody had done it! But they're all saying *I* did it!"

When she found out at last about the pregnancy rumors her family had spread, she was so deeply ashamed and hurt that she tried to kill herself. "I went ahead and took an overdose of sleeping pills. Because I felt there was no purpose, I would have to cut and run. I just didn't want to face it again, I didn't want to live. I felt there was nothing left. But Daddy got me out of it. He made we walk, he stuck me in the shower. I was completely oblivious to anything that went on that night. He took me out with a bunch of friends to this diner, we were sitting way in the back, and I kept falling over on the table. There were two other couples. And he kept saying, 'Sit up. Sit up.' I said to him: 'You're always telling me to lie down and now you're telling me to sit up?'"

This became a family saying; I had heard my mother tell the story often. It was odd that she could banter so openly about her suicide attempt, even make it into a kind of dirty joke. In the course of time, my father, my sister Betty Ann, and I all tried our hand at killing ourselves—unsuccessfully, thank heaven. Suicide attempts became one of our household's bonding agents. In my case, it happened when I was a teenager, and most susceptible to pessimism, after which I converted to stoicism. But to return to my mother's account of that night . . .

"After the others had left, we sat up talking on the steps till dawn. He talked and talked, and the only thing I remember his saying was, 'Everyone has to justify his existence.' I'm not sure what he meant that night, and I'm still not sure. But I think he meant that each of us has a soul, has a spirit, we're not just a grain of sand on the beach to be lost among the other grains of sand. There has to be a reason we're here. You're a person, and you've got to prove, you've got to *be* that person. I think that was the only thing I was awake enough to hear. I let it rattle around in my head. But I didn't want to justify my existence, I didn't want to exist. My family didn't care what happened to me. You think anyone cared if I lived or died? Nobody."

"Well, Dad did."

"I wasn't so sure of that. Maybe to him it was just a challenge. Anyway, at the time I was living with a family, and I realized after I tried it that it wouldn't have been a good thing: it's not nice to commit suicide if you're living in somebody's house."

True. I try to imagine the humiliation my mother felt when she learned the cause of her undeserved sluttish reputation. Shame—particular among the young—can unravel a connection with others, with oneself, and with life itself. She must have felt unworthy of being loved, and much more deeply orphaned than ever before. In retrospect, only the embarrassment and mortification her family felt when she ran away could begin to account for their disgraceful behavior. My father seems to have acquitted himself decently. A taciturn man, whatever he said in his long speech that night must have cost him quite an effort. Her rationalizing it away as being merely a "challenge" says all we need to know about her own incapacity to believe herself loved.

## *Wedding Bells*

"We sort of talked about marriage at that time and we started making plans. And then one day I got a letter from your father: in his inimitable terse language" [he had been a newspaper reporter, and a firm believer in concision] "he decided that he couldn't get married. Like a newspaper headline: Sorry, cannot go through with this, call it off. That was it. Didn't want to get married, no way he wanted to see me, forget it, goodbye. No, wait a minute, what happened? I remember: When I finally did let Daddy do what he had to do, I got pregnant, and had to have an abortion. I had an abortion, *then* he didn't want to see me. *That* was it. Okay. I'd never been brushed off in that kind of language, it just threw me off-balance. I dated other guys. I wasn't terribly thrilled with this one or that one. But again, it put me back into a no-trusting feeling, where I'd been before. Then one day he called and said that he couldn't live without me, and would I please forgive him, and could we please get married anyway? I didn't have any better offers that day, so I said okay. Later on he explained why he had called it off. He got scared because the guys in his group said, 'Oh, Lopey, what do you want to get married for?' Nobody in that crowd was married at the time, everyone was 'free.' What the hell did he want to be free for? He wasn't going out with a bunch of women, he was paying for sex. He'd only gone to whorehouses. So what did he have to gain by remaining single? He had everything to gain by marriage and nothing to lose.

"At the time he was working at Parkside, which was a textile dye factory, for your Uncle Arthur. He always worked for Uncle Arthur. Uncle Arthur was always there to take advantage of him, and give him some sort of crap shit job at the factory. Al had stopped working as a reporter when the Depression started, around 1930, and so many newspapers went bankrupt. I met him in 1937, we got married in '39. I was a young girl and like most young girls I wanted to have fun. I wasn't looking for commitment, I wasn't looking for a man, I wasn't looking to get married. I was afraid of marriage. But then again, I was afraid not to be married. I think that's why I got married. All the other girls from school, from the club, Junior this and Junior that, they all were getting married. I guess I was greedy. If I didn't get married I'd have to work constantly. I figured, Here was a man who had a steady job. All right, so he wasn't the greatest guy. He wasn't the greatest lover. But I didn't know he wasn't the greatest lover, because I had nobody to compare him with. I'd only had sex that one time, in the rooming house in New Jersey.

"As for Al, he was just not that attractive to me. Not physically. After he sent me that letter backing out of the marriage, I used to say 'I'll get even on him. I'll fix him.' And in a way I did get even on him. Then the pendulum swung the other way: he got even on me. And I wound up picking up the shitty end of the stick.

"I had a modicum of talent. I wanted to do something more with my life. I didn't know how to do it, I didn't know where to do it, I didn't know *what* to do. I felt stifled. It seems that when I was younger, every time I tried something I was ridiculed. I was put down. Nothing I did was ever good enough."

One recurrent theme in her telling was that she had been frustrated at every turn. *Thwarted, thwarted, thwarted.* Well, she certainly *was* thwarted, so why do I feel like mocking this assertion? I guess because it doesn't take into account that it was she who dropped out of high school, she who chose to obey her sister, she who opted to marry my father, and not to pursue her dream, etc., etc.

On the other hand, many women in my mother's generation felt thwarted, justifiably so, and the daughters of these women spearheaded the feminist movement, so is my resistance to my mother's lament a typically male chauvinist response, a defensive "Well *I* didn't thwart her, I was too young at the time, and anyway, collective guilt is a bad idea"? More to the point, shouldn't I try to temper my impatience by putting her chagrin in a larger historical context: the millions of women who were kept from realizing their potential?

If I think now about my attempt to go beyond my parents' bitter life narratives (my father regarded himself as a total failure, my mother as having managed only a little success due to being thwarted by others), it seems to me that I kept hoping to see the forces arrayed against them as not necessarily an ineluctable fate, because I needed for my own sake to believe optimistically that one can rise above one's initial disadvantages. That I was able to do so, however, does not mean that my parents had the same chance. Perhaps they were right in thinking the cards were stacked against them, like characters in a Thomas Hardy novel who struggle against the evil destiny that is closing relentlessly in on them. Still, I like to think that while their defeats in life might have been unavoidable, they had the opportunity to gain more wisdom in the process—if nothing else, to resign themselves to circumstances and not continue to blame others or themselves. To relinquish their grievances. But if they had, what if anything would have been left of their personalities? Hard to imagine them without their bitterness.

## *Pop's Family*

"When you were going out with Pop before you got married, were you also meeting his family?" I hear myself asking her on the tape.

"The first time I met his family, they were living someplace near Forest Hills. I went to their home and we sat around the table between Arthur and Doris, and there were Milton and Joel, Arthur's two sons. At that time Joel was the baby, he was five years old. And Joel looked at me and said, 'Gee, you got a big nose.' Which I really needed from a five-year-old. And you know what my future husband did? My boyfriend? He walked over to the kid and shook his hand. That was when I should have picked up my pocketbook and walked out of that house. But I didn't. I held it in, and then I said I didn't want to see him anymore, because he didn't have enough courtesy to chastise a child for being such a brat. Not only that, but at nine o'clock when Arthur was tired, he went upstairs and went to bed. I mean, that was really a wonderful reception for a new member of the family. They never could understand why I couldn't stand them, why I had such antipathy to Arthur, why I couldn't stand Joel. How can a man do that? To bring a young girl, barely twenty years old, into a house and to let a kid, a little snot-nose, say that, how could he do that? And not only condone it, but laugh and congratulate him! And you know what the reason he gave for it was? 'In my family, you gotta learn to be able to take it. You see what they say about my big ears? They say: Oo, contact.' I said: 'That's fine for you. It isn't fine for me.' And to this day, I don't know why I stayed with him. I think the only reason why is that I had such a low self-image that any piece of garbage man was good enough for me at that time."

I had been on her side about my father's tasteless response, until her last remark, which went over the line. "Well he wasn't exactly a piece of garbage, was he?" I said.

"Oh, he certainly was! For me, at that time, I had no right staying with him. He had a low-paying job, he was no bargain, he was a rotten lover. When he had children he was a rotten father. He was no beauty. My family said, 'What the hell are you staying with him for?' They couldn't understand it. I stayed with him because he had a steady job and it was Depression time. If you didn't have a man with a steady job, you never knew when you were going to eat again. As long as he continued to work for Arthur, he had a steady job. And there would be food on the table."

Here I would ask to digress for a moment and state that, as his son, I always thought my father rather good-looking, in a wiry, Jack Palance way, or like the father in *Bicycle Thief*. He was thin with sharp cheekbones and large hands, and he was exceptionally strong, able to lift huge bales at work and to ring the bell at carnivals. He had a glowering stare behind glasses, intent and intense, and he rarely smiled, as befit a man who knew no happiness, though it did make him look rather ghoulish, scary even. A hard worker, he never took a sick day off, and would go in on weekends or work overtime at night if it meant a few extra dollars for his family. He never spent any money on himself, except for the daily newspaper and an occasional paperback. The word that comes to mind is *austere*. He had a Lincolnesque austere handsomeness. But I could never have convinced her that her husband had physical appeal; it was pointless to try. Attraction is not something you can argue another person into.

"Anyway, I had a hard time adjusting to Daddy's family. I remember going to the beach with them when we were first married. And there I was—a knockout. When we were first married, boy, I had a body that would really knock your socks off. I wore a black one-piece bathing suit that didn't leave anything to the imagination. And I had terrific legs: I can prove that by the picture on the wall. There I was at the beach, and I'm saying to myself: 'What am I doing here with these people? I can't stand these people.' And I simply got up and walked away. I walked on the boardwalk, and I watched the dancers. I found a little piece of beach by myself, and lay down and stayed there."

## *The Wedding*

"Could you describe the wedding?"

"We were married in Kew Gardens Jewish Center. We decided to get married in the morning, because there was an afternoon wedding, and the afternoon wedding's family had decorated the chapel very beautifully for their children's wedding. Flowers all over the place, gorgeous! So I had my wedding there, it was a very small wedding, just my sisters and his brothers. Some of our friends came to the ceremony and left. We had no reception. We all went out to eat in a delicatessen. That was my wedding reception. A good part of that was paid for by Arthur. Larly wouldn't pay for it. I didn't have any money. She had already made me sign over my insurance policy, because she wanted to cash it in. She took the money and paid for whatever, an operation, or to redecorate her living room. Anyway, I wasn't that excited on the day of the wedding. I wasn't a virgin, after all, I wasn't going to wear a long white dress. I had a little white dress with a red sash, which drove Larly up the wall, because the red sash and the trimmings would show my scarlet past.

"The wedding was officiated by a young Rabbi I had once had a date with. It had been a double date. The other guy was the one who had invited me, and the Rabbi had invited this other girl. We wound up switching. We took the ferry to Coney Island. He went as far as to put his arm around me, which was okay. We went on some of the rides. And the other girl started in on 'Ooh, these rides are so frightening, I can't do that,' and really it just bothered me. I'm not a diplomat. I can't stand hypocrisy. I can't stand that silly female Protect-Me game that girls play. I guess I was not too kind to her. And that turned off the Rabbi. I wouldn't have been his kind anyway."

"Let's get back to the wedding."

"After the ceremony we went to the deli. It was the same deli where Gladys had been married, but her reception was in the back room where they had a beautiful ballroom and she had a great big Saturday evening catered affair. And I had—deli in the restaurant in the afternoon, because that was what *I* was worth. Daddy said, 'You could have a big reception, or you could have a winter coat and shoes and things that you need. You could have what you want or you could have what you need.' I chose the second. And that was it."

## *A Brief Recap*

Here's the story so far, in Mom's telling: She was the youngest of eleven, the favorite, but her father died, she was unable to call her father back on his deathbed, then a year later her mother died, leaving her orphaned and at the mercy of her unloving older siblings, so she ran away, in the process losing her virginity, came back in defeat, meeting more cruelty and indifference from her siblings, dated various men, worked in a beauty parlor, met my father, learned she had been the subject of false rumors that she had gotten pregnant as a runaway, tried to kill herself, was found in time by my father, he proposed marriage, then retracted the offer, then reproposed, she accepting in a what-the-hell spirit, and they wed, with a measly party at a deli after the ceremony.

## *The Honeymoon*

For their honeymoon they went to a hotel in upstate New York. There, according to my mother, my father got very randy and fucked her many times. She felt nothing, on her part. The big excitement of the honeymoon was that a large dog leapt on her and tried to rape her, but she fended off the beast. Meanwhile my father was too paralyzed to rush to her aid. My mother often told this story of the dog trying to have its way with her, the implication being that at this particular juncture she was such hot stuff no man, woman, dog, or other large mammal could resist her. I am staring at a photograph of my mother taken around this time; she was twenty-one. It's a black and white photo but tinted, so that her lips are red and her cheeks rosy. (By the way, this is something I warn my writing students never to do: to write long absorbed descriptions of their family photos, because almost invariably they presume more emotion and meaning from these images than can be shared by the reader, who feels left out.) My mother's hair is piled high on top, and flares out on both sides, just above her shoulders, and she is wearing a fairly low-cut blouse with a pompom at the base of the v-neck, and a slightly sneering expression, looking off to the right, her top lip curling upward, her eyes level and appraising: all in all, she seems a confident, attractive young woman. You could never guess the layers of insecurity underneath. She is in one of her thinner periods.

I find, when I am summarizing her narrative in my prose, that I feel tender toward her, or at the very least amused, whereas when I quote her verbatim from the tape transcript I am less sympathetic. Now why is that? Because in the first instance I've made her into a character, *my* character, and start to feel affectionately possessive towards her, as I would a protagonist in my novel, whereas in the second case I am once again her captive audience, at the mercy of her open-ended complaining or boasting.

Just by way of comparison, and at the risk of redundancy, let's hear the way she tells the honeymoon, in her own words:

"We had a honeymoon of sorts. We went to the country for a week. We had a room in the Governor Clinton Hotel for overnight. And that was a very interesting experience because there I was, getting into bed, and I see my new husband stretched out, and there's a bedbug crawling across his chest. So I called the front desk, I was very upset, and they changed our room. The next day we went off to the Catskills. It was a nice little honeymoon. I was almost raped by a big dog. I was sitting in a hammock and the dog jumped up and straddled me, with his front paws over my shoulder, and started banging away at my back. It was a big white dog, heavy with long shaggy hair like a Labrador retriever. The only one who could control that dog was the woman at the farmhouse where we were staying. She called him off. And I tell you, your old man stood there petrified. He didn't even say a word!" [laughs] "He couldn't even say, 'Here doggie, here doggie,' he was shitting green! Here I am, screaming, and he didn't move.

"My hero! But I should have known better than to expect anything. I've never been able to depend on him in a bad spot. It's a way of life. From the very beginning I was on my own. I used to say, 'I can always depend on me because no one else is going to help me out.' It seems to be the way it happened all my life. It followed me all my days. I prefer it. There were times when I used to say: I want to be able to be loved, and not necessarily *have* to love back. I want to be loved—for *me.* Not *needed.* Not for what I can do or what I could supply, or even for comfort that I could give someone. Just for being a . . . a lily of the field. And it's just never been my lot. God, if there is a God in His infinite wisdom, has got to have some plan for me, because sure as hell, this life can't be wasted. Because that's what it seems to be."

"Anything else you remember from the honeymoon?"

"Yeah, I got fucked—we fucked in every goddamn place you can imagine. In the corn field, on the hilltop, outside, inside. That man was almost insatiable. If you could say a woman was a nymphomaniac, your father was a nymphomaniac. God, that pecker of his was at half-mast most of the time. Full mast, lots of the time. The only reason I didn't get pregnant on the honeymoon was that we went through lots and lots of Trojans. I think he came with a gross of them and he ran out of them. When we got to the village, he managed to get to the drug store and buy some more. And you know something? I didn't feel a goddamn thing. That was the lousy part. I didn't know what was expected of me. I didn't know what I was expected to feel. He must have thought that volume was what a woman needs. That frequency is what a woman wants. Because once he got home, he was finished. If it was once in two weeks, it was a lot. Cuz he used it all up in that one week. And then he forgot that he had to be a husband—had to be a man."

I wonder at her insensitivity in refusing to consider what I, as my father's son, might be feeling, when she would talk about his inability to satisfy her sexually. Was she consciously performing this ritual humiliation of my father for my benefit, as a provocation, or was this simply the mouthing of her interior monologue, no matter who was present? My brother Lenny, who had only disdain for my father (one more way in which he identified with my mother), has gone out of his way all his life to prove himself the opposite of Albert Lopate, to demonstrate that he is proficient in the sack. I, out of obstinacy, refuse to regard myself as either a superior or inferior lover, and continue to maintain that it depends on the circumstances. I know enough about sexual performance to grasp that it is not just a matter of objective technique: the same person can be a dynamic lover in some circumstances and an uninspired one in others, partly depending on whatever variations one encounters in the other person's affection, response, excitement, indifference, or hostility. My mother felt little passion for my father to begin with, and hence felt nothing in the act, and he in turn did less and less to please her. Thus a vicious circle ensued in the marriage bed.

## *Settling into Marriage*

"What was it like when you got back from your honeymoon?"

"We got married on the eleventh of June, so we rented an apartment as of the first of June. Up until the eleventh, I spent that time fixing it up. As soon as the couch was delivered, and the radio was delivered, Mr. Lopate stretched out and did not get up. I climbed up on the ladder; I put up the window shades, the hooks, and the curtain rods. I learned how to do a lot of things by myself. I would ask for help and never got it. It was unbelievable! I don't know how many times those first couple of months I would say, 'What am I doing here? Why am I going through this?' And it all came down to the same thing: 'You're doing it because he's the only one you know who has a steady job, and it's Depression time.' I'm being honest. Never mind the commitment, never mind the possibility of love afterwards. I knew there was no love. I knew there would never *be* love. But I tried. I hoped it would work. I hoped he would change. I hoped he would be—a good husband. I found he was not. I took my chances: It's like gambling. You put your money down. If it comes up red, fine. If it comes up black, you're shit out of luck."

"I have a feeling a lot of men at that time didn't do housework," I said.

"Yes, it was partly that generation of men. But by that time, the change was already starting. Husbands were already starting to wheel baby carriages, starting to be proud of their children. My husband never took my children to the park in a baby carriage. I don't know why, but . . . Did he ever take you to the park? Did he ever spend time with you?"

"He did spend some time with us, yes."

"All right—did he ever spend the time you would expect of a father? I used to hear, 'Hey, Fran, the baby's crying.' As if I couldn't hear the baby crying. However, some of the changes were really distressing. The first couple of weeks, I would look out the window and see him coming from the bus. And a block before, he would start running, really anxious to get home. And there would be a tub of water ready for him, and he would jump in as soon as he got home. Because he would come home from that factory job with collars of black dirt on his legs and arms that I couldn't stand. And he would get into the tub every night when he came home. For about a week. Afterwards, he would not bother to get into the tub. The water would stand there every night, and he wouldn't bathe. Every night he would come home dirtier and dirtier and dirtier. He couldn't understand why I didn't want him near me. And it got so that I had to reject him—constantly. He smelled. His teeth, his mouth, his legs. It hurts to say these things. It hurts me to say them because I had to tolerate him, and it hurts me to say them because I did tolerate him. He had no idea how tempting it was to bed somebody else. To be able to have someone that I could enjoy, without that awful smell. I guess my getting pregnant was an excuse to have him stay away. And I was able to live without him for a long time, when I was pregnant. It was wonderful. I couldn't understand why he felt the need—what was he holding onto all that dirt for? So much about him I couldn't understand. The way he would come home and listen to the radio. It was always sports, a basketball game or a football game. That hasn't changed over the years. I even had to absorb it: I watch and I know a little bit about sports, from the process of osmosis. But it wasn't pleasant to constantly be a maid. And then of course when Lenny was born, he still wouldn't help me, absolutely wouldn't wash a dish, wouldn't take the laundry over to the launderette. He did nothing! My legs were swollen three times the size of normal, I had such edema it was unbelievable. And the doctor said, 'You must stay with your feet elevated.' You know what my husband did? He brought me a high stool from the factory, so that I should be able to sit and wash the dishes. That's consideration of a sort. But he wouldn't wash the dishes himself."

It's starting to sound like *Sons and Lovers*. When I read that great D. H. Lawrence novel, I thought: Okay I'm not alone, here again is the middle-class woman horrified by her dirty working-class husband, and the sensitive son going back and forth between the two. Except my father was not only a working-class brute but an autodidact semi-intellectual who read Kafka and Dostoevsky. I could imagine him coming home exhausted from the physically draining day at factory work, the sole financial support of his expanding family, wanting only to zone out with a ballgame, and there was his wife, who wasn't working, expecting him to help around the house and do the dishes, and who wouldn't go near him unless he took a bath, proof in his mind that she did not love him, did not care for him enough to embrace him as he was, so out of stubbornness and resentment at being rejected he did not take a bath, and the situation worsened.

Of course in looking at it in this way, I am maximizing sympathy for my father as a generic working-class guy at this stage in history, worn down by labor on the one hand and the complex demands of domestic life, for which he was ill-prepared, on the other. All of which may be true, but what I am not acknowledging sufficiently is that my father *was* peculiar, hermetic, weirdly silent, and withdrawn, especially when he felt himself under attack. Increasingly mocked by us for his morose antisocial manner, he became isolated in his head, expecting not to be understood, and hopeless to reach.

I am well aware that I am not succeeding in making my father come alive on the page, turning him into a three-dimensional character or simply giving a proper account of the man. In part it's because the focus of this book is my mother and her point of view, and in part because I've already written a long personal essay about him ("The Story of My Father," published previously)—though that's hardly a valid excuse. The main reason is that he was so remote and shadowlike in life that I find it difficult to describe him, much less understand him.

In any case, who can blame my mother for being repulsed when he smelled and wouldn't wash? What was that all about? I don't share his need to hold onto body dirt. As for the rest, I too drift into silence at times, and my own family berates me for not being livelier and more present at the breakfast table. I tell myself it's because I'm a writer, and writers are always going off into interior space, writing in their heads. What is more likely is that I'm my father's son, and would have inherited this peculiarly quiet, watchful, impassive way regardless of what career path I followed. In short, it's not a professional deformation, it's genetic. So if I cut my father slack for his introverted oddities, it's probably because I want the same type of slack cut for myself.

"Were you working at the time?" I asked.

"I had quit all my jobs. I had quit everything."

"Well, what did you do in the house when you were alone?"

"While I was pregnant, there was no problem. I used to go to the movies a lot. Once the housework was done I walked out of the house. But I always managed to have a meal on the table. I'd go to the movies. I saw all the musicals. I didn't like the Westerns, but Dick Powell, when he sang—I liked all those big Goldwyn musicals, Busby Berkeley, they were terrific. I liked *The Thin Man,* and the mysteries. The matinee idols I liked were William Powell, Clark Gable, Melvyn Douglas, and of course Leslie Howard. I think I saw *Romeo and Juliet,* with Leslie Howard and cross-eyed Norma Shearer, two or three times. I had a crush on James Mason when I saw him in *The Seventh Veil.* I think every woman sees an unobtainable man that she wants to tame and obtain for herself. And in that picture he was the unapproachable man who was finally won by a young innocent girl. Every time it's on television I watch it. I don't care if there's a ballgame on or not, I have my rights.

"So, besides going to the movies, I'd stop by Butch's gas station and he would take me home in his car. After I had Lenny, I would sometimes bring the baby carriage over to Butch's to visit, and he would put the carriage in the back of his car and drive me home, and always he would say: 'Why can't you lose that guy and come with me? How can you live with him? He's dull, he's terrible. How can you live that way?' It didn't make any impression on me. I didn't leave Daddy, I just wanted a ride home.

"Everything was fine. There was no problem before the babies were born, because there was not a lot of work to do. But once the babies were there, once Lenny was born, forget it! I had my hands full and I had no one to turn to. I remember Al's cousin Suzanne walked into our house one time when Lenny was an infant. She asked me if we were moving. Every stitch was out of the closet, every dish was in the sink, because I hadn't gotten around to doing the dishes. I *couldn't* do it all. I was not an organized person. I never had the experience, I never had the training. I never had anyone teach me how to do it. I was just a kid! Okay, so I was twenty-one years old—that's not a kid, really. But in my head I was a kid. I didn't know anything. But I had a man who was eight years older than I, who at least should have helped. No, nothing. If you're doing childcare, and you have nobody to help you with the other things like housekeeping, it's rough for a kid who never had to do it."

All very true, to which must be added that my mother was a dreadful housekeeper. Her resentment at having to clean without my father's assistance, combined with a certain inability to organize and simplify the piles that accumulated everywhere around us, led to our living in what she termed "a pigsty," long after she had left her twenties behind her.

I am still struggling to adjudicate in my mind my mother's claims of being mistreated in the early stage of her marriage with her testimony that she went to the movies regularly and dropped in on her friend Butch who had a crush on her, while my father was working long hours in a factory. Do I sound naïve by saying it doesn't seem such a bad deal? Being a cinephile myself, I can never fault her going to the movies: It was a great period for American sound pictures, and who could resist Clark Gable, James Mason, and Busby Berkeley musicals? Intellectually, I can grasp the "diary of a mad housewife" scenario and the basic injustice of a sexist social structure that could leave a young wife feeling bereft and adrift. But I suspect there is an emotional divide between women readers who will more readily sympathize with her, and men (or perhaps I should say men like myself) whose compassion keeps straying to the other side, do what we may to compensate for our gender bias. I wish there was a way to correct that astigmatic deviation and leap into her perspective with warmth and wholeheartedness, but my imagination will not take me that far. Such are the limits of a feminist-friendly male, which I consider myself to be, who is nevertheless—a male. What I cannot seem to do is bluff an empathy I do not feel. Instead I keep wanting to convince her to go easier on the guy. Try talking more honestly or less accusatorily; maybe go to a sex therapist. These sorts of remedies occurred to me when I heard them arguing and they still occur to me, even after they are both cremated ashes. It was always too late for reconciliation: the possibility had closed down before I was even born. But the son in me could never stop myself from hoping for a more rational solution or a miracle, some magic transformation of antagonism into affection.

## *Motherhood*

The first baby came a little over a year after they married (the guys in the Jewish Center were counting the months to see if they were less than nine). "I was at the movies Saturday evening with my sister, and around seven o'clock, I got a pain. I didn't know what it was; it seemed like I was having a very severe gas pain. I thought I needed to fart. Before the end of the movie, I got another one. And that night, I started to have labor." She was in intense labor for over a day. "Daddy went to the hospital. The next day, he went to work. My sisters were there but he had left."

"What was it like, giving birth?"

"They gave me ether. It's a painful process, no question about it. Now they have all sorts of exercises. We didn't know from exercises, we didn't know from breathing. You just lay there and suffered. And you cursed your husband for fucking you and getting you pregnant, but you knew you had done it too. But your old man went to work. There was no question of taking a day off—he had to go to work."

"I'm trying to divert you from complaining about Father, so you can tell me what the experience was like for you."

"It was painful, but utter relief once it was over. They told me I had a son. I had wanted a girl, not a boy, because everyone was saying that with a son, once he grows up you lose him, but a girl is your friend forever. My two sisters were crying, 'You have a son, what a beautiful son.' And I said: 'Big deal.' Then the nurse brought the child into me, and I took a look at this boy, he had dimples all over his face and his head was covered with brown fuzz and I said: 'Oh my God, he's gorgeous! That's mine!' And I fell madly in love with him. He made a face that only a mother could love. You know how a rubber face gets contorted, one of those plastic masks that you can push into any shape? He pushed that face into a weird shape and I got hysterical laughing. That was my son, and he was the most beautiful thing you ever saw."

Lenny was over nine pounds, and "the hungriest little bugger." But she couldn't nurse him at first because, in spite of her large bust, her nipples were too small and her milk too watery. Eventually she was able to nurse him but supplemented it with bottles. "Whatever I gave him in that formula made him sick, and I had to bathe him in horse bran. The whole house smelt like a barn. I had to make a teabag out of this stuff I got at the stable, which the pediatrician told me about. It helped. Of course I changed the formula too—whatever it was that was bothering him. He was such a good baby. One time, though, he held his breath, and I picked him up and patted him on the behind and I said 'Stop that!' He looked at me with such surprise and he stopped. He never did it again. I guess he knew who was boss!"

Three years later I was born. "The day after you were born there was an air raid drill. We hadn't been warned, and so instead of pulling all the curtains they turned off all the lights. And all the babies that were being fed with bottles were screaming their heads off. But not my Phillip. I just shoved my bust in your mouth and you drank. Because by that time my nipple had gotten big enough.

"When you were circumcised, you had a bad circumcision. I was afraid you might have bled to death. They had to put a stitch in it. They said: 'You see that little piece of thread hanging out there? That's a stitch.' I was practically on the floor, because my brother-in-law David had had a brother who had died, who had bled to death from a circumcision. But they said, no, it was all right, when they saw you were bleeding too much they put a stitch in it. They said you were okay, the stitch will fall out by itself. As a result, when I took you back a few weeks later for an examination, the pediatrician told me that you have two holes at the end of your penis. Congratulations. When you were very little, you couldn't understand why you peed this way and that. I said, 'For God's sake, aim for the toilet!' You whined: 'I did, but it's on my shoe, Ma.'

"But you were a good baby. Of course compared to Betty Ann, anybody would have been a good baby. She wasn't sickly, she just was a *pisher.* But you had your moments. You used to spit at me. A couple of whacks across your mouth stopped that. I knew something about childcare because I used to babysit for my nieces, Betty and Jane. Childcare was easy, that came naturally to me. You give them love and keep them dry and fed, there's nothing else to do. Teach them right from wrong, tell them never to open their mouth to an older person. That's all."

Was she a good mother? Yes, I think so: "good enough," to use the practical terminology of English psychologist D. W. Winnicott, who counseled that a mother didn't have to be perfect, she could be depressed or angry, but if she somehow was able to shepherd her children into a reasonably intact adulthood without their turning into serial killers or going insane, that was sufficient. Neuroses are a given: as Freud maintained, we're all neurotic. But that doesn't mean that you should keep blaming your parents for fucking you up (*pace* Philip Larkin). I've never been happy for long, but I've managed to stay engrossed, even creative, and to the degree I've lived a productive life, I owe an enormous debt to my mother and her love for us as children, which was never in dispute.

A year after my birth, almost to the day, my sister Betty Ann arrived. "I didn't expect to get pregnant with Betty Ann. But it happened, and I was delighted. I wanted children. I figured: I'm stuck in a marriage. Evidently it's going to be a lousy marriage. But there's no way I'm going to be able to leave him and get a defense job, or go into a plant. Nobody's there to take care of my children. So I'm stuck. I had to have some way of—not necessarily of being creative, but someone to lavish all the feelings and emotions and affection that I had inside me, I had to give it to somebody. Because I knew that if I gave it to him, it was wasted.

"You children were very important to me. I used to figure: Well, someday they'll grow up, and maybe they'll realize my sacrifice. Maybe they won't. If they do, I'll be lucky. If they don't, I'll find a way of managing."

That omnipresent question lurks in almost every parent's mind: *Will they ever realize how much I've sacrificed for them?* My mother wanted us to recognize her sacrifice, consisting mostly of staying in a loveless marriage for our sake; the only problem with this idea is that she continued to stay married to my father for decades after we turned adult. I do acknowledge her sacrifices, both large and small, in raising us, but what she was less disposed to hear was that I also recognized the sacrifices of our father, his slaving away like a donkey to support us, with barely any gratitude expressed from his children in return.

## *The Candy Store*

When Lenny was two, my mother took it into her head to run a candy store. She wanted to get my father away from the ribbon-dyeing factory and his employer, Uncle Arthur. It seems the factory employees were forming a union, which my father, a liberal Democrat, always staunchly pro-union, wanted to join, but he was torn because he also felt loyal to his brother Arthur. Though he essentially functioned as a worker, Arthur designated him, a family member, as "management," which meant he couldn't join the union and he didn't get a raise, like the others. "He got fucked all around. He was in a very bad position: if he wanted to join the union he would be considered to have betrayed his brother." My mother was angry at Arthur from the get-go. I think she saw my father as less than a man for knuckling under to Arthur's wishes. Whether or not Arthur was actually exploiting my father—or "taking advantage of him," as my mother put it—is debatable. Arthur, according to her reluctant testimony, helped my family out with loans from time to time, and it would seem that my father felt safe working for him. Still, there was no love lost between the two men. They had one of those typically acrimonious (going back to Biblical times) Jewish sibling rivalries. Arthur came to exemplify in our family mythology the ruthless, hypocritical man of business, and our father the purer, more downtrodden worker with the soul of an artist.

Here would be the right moment for me, if only I knew more, to weigh in on the actual rectitude or malevolence of Uncle Arthur, whom we visited from time to time in his spacious home in Queens, once in a blue moon (he never came to our house: it was assumed it would be a "treat" for us children to get out of our ghetto and enjoy his backyard with the swing set, if not our snotty cousins who barely interacted with us, perhaps afraid of catching poverty cooties). Arthur himself was a man of few words, showed very little interest in us as individuals, and seemed always mentally preoccupied, which suited me fine. I am trying to say that I did not find him *evil,* the way my mother did, merely distant and self-important. He wore a fedora at all times, in my mind's eye.

So my parents invested in the store, using what little savings they had and borrowing the rest from—Uncle Arthur. Why a candy store? "When we first moved into that neighborhood, we had a little apartment over a fruit store. We were friendly with Sarah and Nat who owned the candy store. And they were having marital problems. She started playing around with the Italian guy next door, Carmine, and her husband started whacking her around. But we were still going over to the candy store for our papers, our sodas, whatever, and also it was a hangout. We had a lot of friends there: guys who finally went in the army. Sarah and Nat just closed the store and disappeared. The store remained vacant, and I was able to buy it very, very cheaply. I think the whole thing came to about twenty-one hundred dollars. We didn't buy the property, we just bought the fixtures. I figured: Here was a business that I can start building up again from practically nothing. Everyone in the neighborhood knew us, and we could make a good living out of it. The apartment was in the back. I didn't have to worry about keeping an eye on Lenny."

"How did you learn the business?"

"What's to learn? We knew how to make an ice-cream soda, we knew how to make an egg cream. We knew how to sell candy. Unfortunately, before we opened the store, it was broken into and all the cigarettes and cigars were stolen. We were babes in the woods; it never occurred to us that someone would steal the cigarettes. At that time, cigarettes were rationed. Ice cream was also rationed. That was a big expense, to replace all that stuff. But the salesmen and vendors were very cooperative. They felt that we would be able to make a go of it, and we did. We built it up from practically nothing to a nice, growing business. We worked very hard. I had two babies in that store, you and Betty Ann. When we first started running the candy store, I did it by myself. Even when I was pregnant with you, Al would work at the store only on weekends and evenings. After you were born, I would still have to get up for a middle-of-the-night feeding. Al would get up early in the morning and open the store, then I would take over and he would go to work. Eventually he quit his job at the factory. But it took a while, because he was loyal to Arthur. Arthur could talk him into anything. I had no influence over him. Finally he came to work in the candy store because he found out the girl that was working there was stealing from us. She put a twenty-dollar bill in the register, and all of a sudden it wasn't there. Mainly he decided to leave Arthur when it got to a point that it was either leave or lose me. Well, he had almost lost me anyway, because there was somebody who used to come in the store, who was crazy about Betty Ann, crazy about you, this wonderful Italian man, who would have given his right arm and pay anything for me to divorce Daddy and marry him. He saw what was going on."

"What do you mean, what was going on?"

"I don't know if I told you about the time on Mother's Day: We used to sell boxes of candy, Whitman's Samplers, and cards, and elaborate presents, and—I was a mother. The guys used to come in and they would tease Daddy. This one time they teased him: 'What did you get for Fran? What did you get her for Mother's Day?' And he said: 'She's not my mother.' He never got me anything. Finally they teased him to the point that he went out and got a bouquet of flowers, and he went to the back where I was taking care of all the babies. He brought it into me and I took a look at it and I went out into the street, picked up the top of the garbage can and dropped it in. I didn't even acknowledge it. That's the way I felt. If you have to have people pressure you into doing something for your wife—I didn't appreciate it. I was tired of being an afterthought. To me it was always too little and too late."

That was my mother's mantra: too little, too late. She could never resist an Anna Magnani operatic gesture like throwing flowers in the garbage. Of course it might have been better for all concerned if she had accepted his bouquet with a simple thanks: it might have even encouraged my father to start giving gifts regularly. But she would never second-guess herself when it came to getting even. Me, I am a firm believer in The Positive Reinforcement School for Husbands: If you resent your husband for not doing the dishes, when he does do the dishes compliment him profusely, instead of picking apart his performance, and he may make it a habit.

My father was, true enough, not a big present-giver: I don't remember any of us ever receiving birthday gifts from him. When he died, this failure to buy us presents was brought up as proof that he was a no-good, though for some odd reason it never disturbed me. My mother also was not a particularly generous present-giver, though I assume that had to do with our straitened financial circumstances. The long and short of it is that, when we were growing up, presents were not a big part of our family culture.

To continue my mother's account:

"I guess the only reason why I didn't leave him was that I wasn't crazy about that Italian. His name was Tony, I think—Tony or Vinny—what else? He was a nice guy. He would put you and Betty Ann in the carriage, and take Lenny by the hand, and walk around the block. With Al, no matter what I did, it was never good enough. No matter how much I tried to be a wife, an attractive wife—I sang, I danced, I always dressed nicely, my hair was always clean, I was always clean—it was never enough. I don't know what he wanted from me. Maybe I wanted too much."

"It doesn't sound like he was complaining it wasn't good enough, it sounds like you were the one complaining."

"I tried to set an example. I would bathe, I would brush my teeth, I would change my clothes. I would do things to be *alive*. It didn't make any impression. I tried to get him to go back to school, when we first moved to Brooklyn, after we got rid of the store. He had so much intelligence, the intellect was spilling over, and yet he had mental onanism. It was being wasted!"

Back in the mists of time, when he was in his twenties, my father had entered college, taking classes at night and working days, but he was too exhausted to keep his eyes open in class and do homework in the early morning before going off to his job, so he dropped out of school. After that, he contented himself with being an autodidact, reading books and newspapers at spare moments, doing the crossword puzzle every day. He collected stray bits of arcane information and liked to show off his knowledge—the less useful, the better.

"Your father wasn't doing anything with his brain. Betty Ann used to say he's the greatest living vegetable: too bad we can't eat him. He liked movies until after we got married, then he didn't want to go anywhere. He became married to his chair and his radio. He didn't like nightclubs. The only time he went out to a nightclub was when we had the store. We used to close one day a week. We had a babysitter and we had someone to make sure the store was locked up, and we would go out. We went to an Israeli nightclub called Sabra. It was fun. But we also went to theaters on the night when we were closed, and stage shows."

There was a photograph I used to stare at of my parents in a nightclub, sitting at a big white table with two rolls of revelers smiling at the camera, my father grimly staring, my mother looking shiny with pleasure and anticipation, ready to jitterbug.

"After we were married, I joined a record club that sent out classical music albums. What he brought home to me were records I didn't like. I didn't like that jazz and those blues, because to me it sounded like whining. I can't stand people who whine, and I can't stand music that whines."

Being an incurable devotee of jazz and blues, I let her irritating comments on them pass. "Where did the habit of disliking whining come from?"

"I think it came from myself. You see, I consider myself a sculptor, having to sculpt a person out of nothing. I regarded myself as a blob, because there was nobody to give me a background. I was never able to sit at my grandfather's or grandmother's knee and learn their wisdom. I envy these people who have had their personalities shaped by somebody not themselves. So whatever I am, I've had to create myself."

The truth is, my mother had been exposed to classical music by her father. I've always mistrusted this notion of self-invention, which seems ungrateful, not to mention ahistorical. I'm sure my mother's values were shaped to a large extent by her parents and even by her siblings. As for me, I keep trying to trace how deeply I have been marked by family influence. Here I'm speaking less of childhood wounds than cultural inheritance. It was enough for my taciturn father to throw out recommendations of Faulkner, Bessie Smith, and Stroheim's *Greed* for me to begin to acquire a literary, jazz, and film culture, while my mother's subscription to the classical music monthly album club exposed me to Bach, Mozart, Stravinsky, and Gershwin. My brother introduced me to Charlie Parker, Billie Holiday, Rogier van der Weyden, Piero della Francesca, and many other treasures. So how can I ever claim to be self-invented, even if I were tempted to?

But I suspect that my acknowledging of debts to forbears is less a matter of humility than self-approval. Boasting is one of the Lopates' consistent family traits. That, and the valuation of intelligence above everything, including kindness. Not that kindness did not exist in my family; just that it was never spoken of highly. To appreciate it as the supreme virtue it is, we four siblings would each need to go outside the family and learn it from our mates.

## *Grandpa*

"What was your relationship like with Daddy's father, Grandpa?"

"Around the time I met your grandfather I met some people from the shul that he was associated with in Jamaica. And I heard a young man say: 'If that man Samuel Lopate ever comes near my little sister, I'll kill him!' Grandfather was a well-known—toucher of young women's brassieres. He used to sit and talk to me and he'd be patting me on the breast. He acted like he was getting my attention, but he could have got my attention by touching my arm, by touching my face, touching my shoulder. No, he had to touch me on the breast. And I threw him out of the house eventually. I had to, because he was a hypocrite and a rotten person. I think he had a lot to do with my husband's neuroses and *mishegas*. A lot of things he did I will never forgive him for—any more than I will forgive my family for what *they* did to me. When his third wife Esther was in the hospital, dying, both Daddy and Arthur came to the hospital. And Samuel walked up and down the hall, met some friends and he said: 'These are my sons.' He put his arm around Arthur and said: 'Isn't he beautiful?' And there was Albert standing there, with a sad face hanging out. His father didn't pay any attention to him. That old fucker only worshipped one thing: money, and anyone who could make money. Arthur could make money, so he was beautiful."

My mother's mixture of pity and disdain for my father remains confounding. They obviously had something in common when they started out: both were orphans, or quasi orphans, estranged from their families, feeling unloved. That sympathetic bond obviously had a shelf life, but traces of it lingered, so that in the midst of my mother's harshest statements about my father, she would suddenly express compassion for him by thinking of his family and hating them even more.

"We had Grandfather living with us for a while. He had to go somewhere. So we said, 'Keep an eye on the kids,' since both of us were working in the store. Betty Ann was maybe eighteen months old, and she used to sit in the back in the store and say 'Grandpa, come here! Gotta see ya!' She had a mouth on her. *You* didn't talk. You didn't have to. You were saving it up for your typewriter."

"I always thought Grandpa was a man of means. Why did he have to move in with you?"

"Grandpa had some money, but he would stash it away and cry that he didn't have any. So we took him in. Arthur didn't want him. Doris, Arthur's wife, wouldn't put up with him. He couldn't get on with Doris at all. He stayed with Arthur and Doris for a while, but they put him out. What bothered him was that Doris would take the teabags and dry them out and use them again." [laughs]

"Didn't he have a house of his own?"

"No. When Daddy's mother died, she left all her money to the children she had had with her first husband: Blanche, Charlie, and Bernie. And she didn't give two shits in hell for your old man. She didn't care anything about Arthur and Grandpa at all. So they went ahead and sued. But Daddy had too much pride to sue. He said, 'To hell with it. If you feel that way about me, I don't need anything from you.' Arthur didn't feel that way. But by the time he got around to suing, the statute of limitations had run out, and all they got was a pittance. The old man got something from Esther, his third wife. She was a nice lady."

"So what was it like living with Grandpa?"

"I used to think that a man who was so well-versed in religion could give you the answers. But if I asked him why something or other was the way it was, the only answer he had for me was 'It's written in the book.' There was never any reason behind what he said. He was not a wonderful person. He used to sit in the back and snooze. He could fall asleep on a kitchen chair. He and Bernie would come and visit. He would sit at the table and go fast asleep. Bernie would be sitting on the other side, fast asleep. Daddy would be stretched out in the living room on a chair, fast asleep. These were the men in my family.

"I threw Grandpa out of the house, because he didn't come to your bar mitzvah. His excuse was that he couldn't ride on the Sabbath. But it was all right for him to ride on Shabbos when he went to the theater. Or go to Arthur's son's bar mitzvah. When he came finally on a Sunday, after your bar mitzvah, I told him he could turn right around and get out. I said I didn't want him in the house anymore, wanted nothing to do with him. If the children wanted to see him, they could come see him on their own. If my husband wants him here, let him speak up. Al didn't say anything, so I took it for granted he didn't want him there either. The only thing I ever got out of your grandfather was aggravation. And an allergy. I thought I was allergic to the weeds in the empty lot when we used to go and visit him. But somehow or other, when I walked past the same lot after he was dead, I never sneezed. That's how I figured out I was allergic to him."

## *The End of the War*

During these taping sessions, my mother would drift inexorably into bitter recriminations against my father. It was the obsessive leitmotif in her narrative, as though every dissatisfaction in her life could be ascribed to having married the wrong man—although sometimes she seemed to shrug him off as an insignificant gnat who barely mattered. Partly to get her off this track and partly because I was at least as interested in the history surrounding her, I would ask about how she responded to major events: in this case, the end of World War II in 1945.

"Well, everyone was very excited. There was dancing in the streets and the sidewalks. People were going crazy, cars were riding up and down. And somehow or other, I don't know why it grabbed

Daddy the way it did, but he just wanted to throw things. I don't think he meant to hurt anybody. It was just his excitement. He got a crate of rotten tomatoes from the fruit stand next door, and started throwing at the cars as they went by. I think it was to test his aim more than anything else, which was pretty bad because he was missing most of them, except that he managed to hit one. It was the wrong one, because the car went around the block and came back, and the man got out of the car and came into the store and grabbed him by the front of his coat and beat him into the ground. The man was saying, 'What are you doing this for? I'm not your enemy.' He couldn't understand why Al did it. And I don't think your father understood why he threw the tomatoes. Afterwards, people kept coming by in the store and giving him rather odd looks."

Hearing this about my father both startled me and didn't. I almost never saw him respond with euphoria or excitement to anything. He wore a stolid mask; you had no idea what he was thinking. But there were moments when he would erupt if sufficiently provoked, and his rare shows of anger were all the more scary because they came across as a spasmodic seizure. It was part of what made him seem alien. Years later he did have something like an epileptic attack, although it was never fully diagnosed as epilepsy, and I never saw it and have only my mother's word to go on: They were on vacation in Florida when he suddenly . . . Oh well, I have no idea what actually happened, except the way the story came down to me was that my mother thought he had died and started to close his eyes prematurely, the way you do with a corpse, when my father bestirred himself. It was one of several occasions when my father suspected my mother of trying to hustle him into the Underworld before his time. As for the tomato incident, who the hell knows? He had gotten a draft deferral from the Army as the father of several children, but perhaps he felt bad about that, felt he had been missing something important the rest of his generation had gone through, and so the tomatoes were like substitute grenades he was hurling at the Nazis.

"How did *you* react to the end of World War II?"

"I had a very . . . distant feeling about the whole war. I was so wrapped up in myself and my pregnancy and my babies that the whole war went by me. I was going around in a coma. I was concerned with food stamps, getting my meat from the butcher. I was concerned with rationing. But I wasn't touched by the war. I would see the pictures in the newspaper and in the newsreels. But my feet used to hurt so badly, that the one night a week I gave myself to go to the movies I didn't care if all of England were set on fire. I didn't care if France fell to the Martians, let alone Germany. It didn't bother me. I was completely absorbed in my own problems. I knew what was going on. I didn't have any immediate family in Germany, so concentration camps didn't touch me. I found out later that I might have had family in Germany. It could be, I never checked. It's not that I didn't care. It's just that I didn't have the energy to care. When one of the boys who hung around the candy store went into the Army, well—I was sad, because he didn't buy his ice cream every day. He sent me pictures, he sent me souvenirs, and when he came home wounded, I was relieved. But the war went past me. During it I gave birth to two babies, you and Betty Ann. I had the store. And my feet were hurting me. Daddy didn't quit his job until it was absolutely essential. When the war was over, it meant that we could get candy and cigarettes again to sell people. But that was the extent of my caring about the war. When I think back, if anyone else had told me they felt that way, I would have been appalled. I have no excuse, except I had too many problems for too young a person; remember, I was only in my twenties.

"One of the guys who hung around the store, Tony, died in the war. He lived upstairs. He was having an affair with a young Italian kid around the corner. He was the brother of the one we used to call Schwarze Rosie, because they were a Sicilian family that were dark enough that if you didn't catch them in the light, they looked Negro. He got killed and . . . his sister Rosie was blaming my neighbor Yetta Levy. She came and started throwing stones at Yetta's house because *her* son didn't get killed. Of course I couldn't understand *that* because Yetta Levy's son was in the hospital with jungle rot on his legs; he had no skin up to his thighs. But he was still alive. The other guys who hung around the store all came back. They went to work. They all got married and picked up their lives. But the woman who was having an affair with Tony, she broke up with her husband, and even though Tony didn't come back, she never got back together with her husband again. She moved away. From her, I got my big roasting pan—I got a lot of things from her. She gave away everything that she couldn't sell. But the war was like a bad dream. Not even a bad dream, just like a dream. It didn't exist. Now when I think of the Holocaust, I feel it much more deeply. Not then."

"And then when the refugees started arriving?"

"The refugees that came in didn't help the situation because their attitude was: 'You don't like my face? Fuck you. You don't like me? I don't like you either.' They were always argumentative. I can understand them now, but I was like too many people at that time. I thought: 'You think you're owed a living because you came out of a concentration camp? I don't owe you anything. Your arrogance doesn't do you any favors. Don't get snotty with me because you came out of a concentration camp. I didn't put you there.' There was one family that moved in, always with a chip on their shoulder, ready to show the tattoo on the arm, always ready to tell what they went through, until it got to be a bore. I didn't want to be involved. I was cold. They *were* difficult to deal with, but I wasn't mature enough to deal with them the way they should have been dealt with. They came here expecting compassion and warmth and love. And—I didn't have it for them. I wasn't receptive. Now I feel guilty. But I'm not going to carry that guilt around the rest of my life."

## *Enough about Him*

On the tape recordings, my mother spent a considerable while telling fond stories about my older brother Lenny: how precocious he was, what an adorable imp, how he used to steal into the store in the early morning and make a breakfast of his favorite candies . . .

Finally I couldn't take it anymore. I asked her, "What was I like as a little boy?" Perhaps the whole point of this interviewing exercise had been to find out how my mother perceived me.

"You were so cute. You were so unbelievably beautiful, and when I would set you out in your carriage outside the store, the women who walked by would look at you and cross themselves because you looked like the infant Jesus. The store still had an Italian name on the awning, and they must have thought you were Italian. You were so beautiful, with those big eyes. Do you remember the time you cut your eyelashes off?"

"Because I thought you loved me only for my eyelashes."

"As though all I could love you for was your eyelashes! And they grew back, thank God! When we lived on Broadway, when you were a little boy, you had a habit. You would take your toys and put them in a paper bag, and you would hold it almost cuddling, and walk from one end of the apartment to the other. This was your routine, your ritual. The time you had your cowboy hat, nobody dared touch that cowboy hat. Until you insisted on wearing it in the tub, then it fell off and made the whole tub red, because it was dyed red, and we finally had to throw that away, and you replaced it with a baseball cap. You wore that to sleep in, you wore it to bathe in, you would not take it off. You were tenacious. You got hold of an idea, some sort of concept that only you knew about, you held onto it. No one could take it away from you, until you were ready to give it up. For a while you were Black Beauty. I would say 'Goodnight, Phillip,' but no, I had to say 'Goodnight, Black Beauty.' You had that stubborn personality trait, and no one was going to get you to change your opinion.

"For the most part you were very easygoing, but occasionally you had a very bad temper. When we were in the country you grabbed Lenny's glasses off his face and threw them into the bushes, and we couldn't find them. We had to send back to the city for a new pair of glasses. Lenny couldn't see; he was walking around half-blind. But when it came to Betty Ann, you had a great deal of patience. Betty Ann was a real pain in the ass. She would wake up in the middle of the night, and she would kvetch and cry and noodge you, because you slept in the same bed with her. She would hit you. And hit you. And you would take it and not respond. She noodged you until you finally sat up and belted the shit out of her, and she really started to howl. Then you lay down and went back to sleep. She got the message to leave you alone. You handled her very well that way and you'd think she would learn, but she did that to you all the time, pester and pester. You had a very high boiling point with her. With everyone else you had a very low boiling point. I used to watch that and wonder: Maybe it's the fact that you and Betty Ann were born so close together, you were both Scorpios. With Lenny you had no patience at all. But your relationship with Lenny was still very good: you were pals. I didn't always insist that he take you wherever he went. And I think that helped. He didn't mind so much taking you places.

"We sent you to Hebrew School. And you had a crush on your Hebrew School teacher. She adored you. Your teacher at the nursery school also adored you. All your teachers loved you. You were a charmer from the word go."

"Why would you think of that as being a charmer? It sounds so insincere. Why not that I was attuned to adults, I liked adults a lot?"

"But you knew how to charm them; that's what I mean. You knew the right buttons to push. You knew how to be nice. In fact, when you got older, in high school you got elected Chief Justice of the Student Court, and you thought you wanted to go into politics because you knew how to argue like an attorney, you knew how to get around people—of course, then you found you didn't want to be an ass-kisser for the rest of your life, so you didn't go into politics—but we always thought that you would run for office, because you just knew how to get to people. You were really quite good at it, from when you were very little."

Already I'm bored, I've heard enough about my child-self. I knew this part fairly well; there were no new revelations.

## *The End of the Candy Store*

"Why did you give up the candy store?"

"I got meningitis, and we had to sell out. Daddy couldn't take care of it himself. When I got meningitis, I was in the hospital for a while. That's when I started to know who my friends were, too. Betty Ann was a baby, you were a little boy. My sister Gladys took Lenny because he wasn't a problem; he was a big boy already. You were two-and-a-half. You were not toilet-trained. You used to shit in your pants. Let's call a spade a spade: there's no sense being delicate about it. Nobody wanted to take care of you because of that. The one person who rose to it, who was crazy about you and didn't really care, was a cousin of Daddy's. Her name was Dorothy Kaplan. She lived across the street from my sister Larly. She said: 'He's absolutely wonderful, he is gorgeous, he's divine. All he does is sleep and shit but I adore him.' She took you for the couple of weeks that I was in the hospital. My sister Dorothy took Betty Ann, and because Betty Ann was a baby she cried. She was in a strange house with strange people. Dorothy brought Betty Ann back, tossed her in Daddy's lap and said no one could take care of her. And then when I got out of the hospital, Daddy collapsed, which was understandable: He was trying to keep the store open and he wasn't used to taking care of a baby and shopping and doing everything, and he ran himself into a state of exhaustion. By the time I came home, he was ready to resign. So we sold the store. Some people came by and paid almost twice as much for it as we had paid initially, because we had built up a nice business. We took the money and found a place in Brooklyn. And Daddy went back to work for Arthur.

"We didn't want to start a new candy store. At that time I thought: Here's a good opportunity for you to get another job. *Don't* go back to Arthur. There are a million jobs out there. The war was over. He had experience in so many different things. But he said: 'Fran, the war is over and the men are coming back, so what do they need me for?' He went back to Arthur. That was it. I knew when he went back to Arthur that that was the beginning of the end. He was never going to get out of there."

## *Williamsburg*

With three children in tow, my mother recounted, it was difficult to rent a new apartment. No one wanted to rent to people with babies. My mother said she told lots of lies—that Lenny was in high school and I was in public school—but to no avail. The housing shortage after the war meant that property owners had their pick, and large families were undesirable. She was so desperate, as she put it, that she would have gone to Harlem. Finally they found a three-bedroom apartment in Williamsburg, facing the elevated train.

At the time, Williamsburg was a shabby Jewish slum, with run-down tenement buildings, and the block we were living on was perpetually cast in semidarkness from the shadows of the elevated train. I remember it as pretty awful. There were rats in the basement, and sometimes one of them would make its way up to the bedroom I shared with my brother. But my mother saw it differently: she said the rear was flooded with sunlight, overlooking a backyard that we kids could play in or climb up the telephone pole to peek in at next door neighbors.

No longer small shopkeepers, we had finally and definitively descended to the working class, and it was appropriate that we live in a ghetto.

"We lived on the third floor. On the first floor was a sewing factory that manufactured gloves, with Russian operators—men, not women. On their breaks, they would take chairs and sit out in the hallway and smoke those blackened, strange-smelling cigarettes, which were probably not marijuana, just strong Russian cigarettes. They always had beards down to their bellybuttons. And then of course there was the landlady, Mrs. Eisenstein. We lived up over her. Mrs. Eisenstein was like a Disney character of a crone. She was small and skinny, with gray hair pulled back in a bun, always wore an apron, and she used to call her son-in-law *Stand-ly*, and her son, *Hen-dry*. She had a married daughter who was a schoolteacher, tall and fat, and a granddaughter, who at that time was in high school. Nice sweet little girl with bad skin with a whiny voice. And the son-in-law was a good-looking man. I could see why she married him, and I guess he married her because there was money in the family. He had a store on the next block, some sort of a hardware store. It was a thriving business. They had real estate.

"As soon as Betty Ann was three and you were four and Lenny was seven, I found out about the First Hebrew Day Nursery. I went and registered you there. They sent a young man to our house who came to investigate. He came up the stairs, sat in the kitchen, and looked at our life insurance policy, said we were very wise, and accepted us. You kids went to the daycare nursery, and I went to work. I started off part-time. I was at Hearn's as a salesgirl, because I had no education. I'd quit school when I was fifteen years old. I didn't know anything. I just did what I had done before: worked as a salesgirl again. Then I . . . got pregnant. But that was another story."

## *The Big Love*

"I think now I've accomplished whatever it is I set out to do. I've sculpted some sort of person out of the blob I felt I started out to be. Probably my greatest accomplishments are my children. My next accomplishment was the fact that I was able to make people happy by being on the stage. What else? I have things inside me, feelings I can't express. Needs I can't fulfill.

"I had love. That will never happen again. That made me very happy when I did have it. I had a great love. One real great love. And that had to suffice me all my life. I guess that's the only thing that helped me put up with the lack of love that I felt for my husband."

After their candy store business had wound down, my parents decided to take a summer vacation in one of those Catskills bungalow colonies, called *kuchaleins,* that lower-middle-class Jews frequented at the time. My father had returned to work at his brother Arthur's factory, and they all drove upstate in one of the company's pickup trucks. This was before the national highways had been built, so the trip was long and the roads narrow and bumpy. My father sat in the front with the driver, his coworker, and my brother Lenny, while my sister and I, aged three and four respectively, bounced around in the open cab in back with my mother. My mother implored my father to switch with her so that she could sit in the front for a while and he could take over the child-watching, but he wouldn't. No doubt he felt it would look unmanly for him to do so, that his place was in the front with the other man, where he often rode shotgun for deliveries, and perhaps he didn't like the idea of his flirtatious wife sitting next to his coworker while he was in the back. "His excuse was, he had to tell the driver how to go." Possibly he did, but my mother didn't see it that way: "Every mile was making me angrier. By the time we got up to that place in Monticello, I was capable of murder. Justifiable homicide. I was a crazy woman, twenty-eight, closer to thirty, and ready to kill. His lack of sensitivity was not to be believed." She stewed over that truck ride, which likely gave her the impetus and justification for what she subsequently did.

They arrived at the site, and shared a big bungalow with two other renting families whom they were meeting for the first time. The bathroom was shared by both families. My brother Lenny got a bad poison ivy rash from wandering bare-assed into the woods, and the other families took to putting corrugated cardboard with a hole cut into it over the toilet seat so that they would not be similarly infected. "They made us feel like lepers." It was the usual messy encounter of city folk with nature, but eventually everyone settled down to vacation. My father played cards with the other men (he was a phenomenal cardplayer, used to earn money at it, could visualize the other players' hands after a few discards), and he went back to his job during weekdays, commuting upstate on Friday night and leaving Sunday, which suited my mother fine.

"All I did all week long was take care of you kids. It was not necessarily a very restful thing, because I was always afraid you guys were going to wander off. It was bad enough that Lenny had his poison ivy and I had to take him to the doctor, who told me to put calamine lotion constantly on it."

"I got lost up there too." It was one of my earliest memories: I had wandered by myself into the mouth of the forest, and suddenly was completely disoriented, leafy hostile Nature surrounded me, and all I wanted was to get back to civilization. Even then, a city boy. I don't remember how I found my way back to the bungalows, or if someone brought me back, but the experience of finding myself lost I now regard as the birth of my self-consciousness. No harm done.

"It's possible. I don't remember. Benno was there with his mother and his stepfather and his sister. He used to go swimming. I tried to get him to practice. He would say, 'Ya, I go.' That was the extent of his speaking at first. I knew that he liked music. I loved music. Here I was, a lonesome woman. My husband didn't pay any attention to me. At that time I had lost a lot of weight. I was twenty-eight years old, and I was very shapely, very attractive, even with the nose, and I had breasts that didn't quit. There was a lot of attraction there between the two of us. And his mother sensed it and probably told him to keep away from me. Benno was exactly the same age as I am. He was German. He had come from a very wealthy family. His father had died of tuberculosis, and his mother remarried into a wealthy manufacturing family. When his stepfather Hymie was put into a concentration camp, his mother, who had managed to escape Germany at the time, was able to buy his way out of the country with thousands of American dollars. By that time Benno had been sent on a plane to the Argentine on a student visa. Once he was in Argentina, he had to wait as a teenager for his number to come up in order to emigrate to America.

"He was what they call a man for all seasons. He was a very macho, masculine kind of man. And I was impressed, because not only was he physical, he was also intellectual. At home I had the intellectual, but I didn't have the physical. I needed a little of each, and Benno had it all. With all the attraction between us, of course there was nothing much we could do about it. We tried very hard not to let it go any further, and we succeeded. The whole summer was just fun, friendly, nice. Daddy would come up—I have pictures of Daddy sitting on Benno's shoulders—he would come up with his bundle of laundry. That summer, all I did was wash clothes. I would spend the whole day Saturday doing laundry and cooking for the weekend, while he'd sit and play cards. He never watched the kids, he never gave me a day off. All I did was work hard, and yet when we got into bed he wanted to screw just the same. And he couldn't understand why I was so reluctant. He never understood me anyway. Now he doesn't even want to, which is unfortunate because we might have had a marriage if he had taken the trouble to understand."

"You said Father was intellectual and not physical. Yet Father was very strong at that time, so what do you mean exactly by physical?"

"What's the good of being strong enough to pick up a bale of ribbon, if you're not strong enough to pick up your wife and hug her and kiss her? I mean physical in terms of affection, loving, and holding your hand, and helping you down off a ladder. Anyway, the rest of the summer went like that. Benno used to dive under the water and grab me by the ankles when we were swimming. He would frolic in the pool. He would *do* things. Everything that Daddy wasn't, he was. And he would sit and listen to music. At least it wasn't the basketball game every time. He wasn't a spectator on life: he tried to be a participant. He was a voracious reader. He didn't speak English very well, but he read English. He was always reading Upton Sinclair. He was pretty much a Socialist. He would read English books, trying to improve his vocabulary because he couldn't talk it too well. His sister married an Englishman eventually when she got back; she married her boss. His sister was a beautiful girl, looked like Sophia Loren. When we got back, Benno went to work as a furrier." [The very same job as her father's, which she did not comment upon, nor even seem to notice.]

"Anyway, we came home. The summer was over. And the basketball games started on the radio, and the football season started. If I wanted to listen to something that wasn't a football game, I had to go and sit in the kitchen and listen. I felt like I was the maid. I started to resent it more and more. I felt I wasn't living in a marriage, I was living with a boarder, who was demanding what I couldn't give him. I used to give it to him, but I didn't want to. I would sleep with him, but it was very reluctant. Anyway, I started taking walks. I didn't know anyone in the neighborhood. The only one I knew in Williamsburg was Benno's mother. So after a while I'd go over to their house, spend a half-hour or so, and then leave. His mother didn't like it. 'Oh, her again.' I knew it, I felt it, but I was so desperate, I had to do something, I had to go somewhere. I was the loneliest woman in the world. All I had was a bunch of sleeping children, and a husband who didn't pay me the slightest bit of attention. And I didn't have enough money to go to the movies every night.

"Well, 1947, the day after Christmas, they had forecast snow flurries. That day it snowed and snowed. Twenty-seven inches of snow flurries. I took you guys out on sleds, bundled you up. Lenny and I would pull the sled, and you and Betty Ann, bundled up, were sitting on the sled. Betty Ann had such a round body she kept on falling off. And she would laugh and laugh, and you would laugh." [I actually remember this sled adventure as one of the happiest times of my childhood, little suspecting the romantic interlude also transpiring.] "There was no traffic. The snow was too deep even for the trolley cars to run on Broadway. I walked all the way down to Havemeyer Street and did some shopping at whatever stores were open, just to walk. My lungs felt so clean and so clear and the snow kept falling down and I felt so young, and I came back home and ran up the stairs and the four of us, the three kids and me, laughed and laughed and we thought we were never going to stop laughing. It was just delightful. I put all of you into hot water, and you took hot baths, and I got you dressed up all nice and snuggly, and I put you to bed. Daddy came home, and he turned on the basketball game.

"I couldn't take it anymore. I thought: I gotta get out. I had to have an excuse to go over there. So I got together some phonograph records. And of course I took Old Faithful, the one record I knew would drive any man crazy, Ravel's *Bolero*. We were always having arguments: the classics versus the moderns. I wouldn't say that Ravel was modern, but that was as modern as I was going to get at that time. That and Stravinsky. But I figured I'd leave the Stravinsky at home, and bring the Ravel. I came out of the house and the snow had stopped. Everything was quiet. You know how it is after a snow, when everything's quiet? There was still no traffic, and the whole sky was black and shining, and all the stars were out, you could see everything, the moon was big, and it was just—breathtaking. And the only thing that bothered me was the yellow dog's pee on the snow.

"I followed somebody's footsteps in the snow and I got to his house. He was home. I didn't know that his parents had gone the day before to Florida. He was alone. And we sat around, talked. Then he played his Tchaikovsky and I took out my Ravel. We talked, and I said Okay. I started putting my boots on, and he took my boots off. And one thing led to another. And another. And then I knew what I was expected to feel, when a woman has sex. What it's supposed to be."

"What do you mean, what you were expected to feel?"

"Having sex with Daddy, I never knew what it was supposed to be. I didn't know what I was supposed to feel. I only knew that he was feeling something, otherwise he wouldn't be keeping doing it. I knew that when he had orgasms, he was coming because he had some feeling. I never had that. I thought, This is it? Shit, if that's sex, who needs it? But with Benno it was different. For one thing, he wasn't a missionary. And he had technique. Because he had a small penis, he used everything. I never knew what cunnilingus was until he did it. And I was going out of my mind. I didn't know such things existed. I didn't know I could feel that way. I didn't know I was *permitted* to feel that way. I didn't know if God meant me to feel that way. I said, it must be, otherwise I wouldn't have felt that way. I just sat back and enjoyed it.

"I came home. The basketball game was just over. And I sat there in the living room, all nice and warm and cozy inside, with my mind and my heart still over there. There was my husband standing there describing every play of that basketball game. Who hit the basket, who missed the shot. Why? I don't know. Maybe he thought I'd be interested. And you know, I felt sorry for him. Even at that time. I said to myself, 'Poor fool. You're trying to reach me.' He must have been trying to reach me. He must have known something had to have happened. Because I was not there. Involved as he was in his basketball game, he had to have sensed something. He was trying to batter his way into my mind, and he didn't know how to do it. He took the wrong way, because it was only his way. He always said he was proud of the fact that we had communication. We didn't have communication. We had lectures. He always lectured me. He talked and talked and talked. And it was up to me to listen. Because I never had any answers for him. He always had the upper hand."

"So what happened after that with you and Benno?"

"Well, we found places to go. It was wintertime, but his cousin went on vacation, so we used his cousin's apartment once a week. And then I was to babysit for my sister Gladys's kid. He would come over there. We managed. It wasn't until June that I realized I was pregnant. When I became pregnant with Joannie, Daddy started seeing a lawyer, and the lawyer contacted me and told me that my husband was going to sue for divorce, and he's going to take away the three children, and if I wanted to keep the fourth child, I could, but the first three he was going to take away."

"How did you know it wasn't Daddy's?"

"I knew, because he was always careful, and Benno wasn't."

"I don't know how to put this, but . . . why wasn't Benno careful and why didn't you make Benno be careful?"

"Because I didn't care. It's as simple as that. Of course I knew it might happen. I asked Daddy for a divorce. I told him I had slept with someone and I wanted to leave him. Adultery was the only grounds for divorce in New York State at that time. When he said he was going to take the three of you away, I couldn't do it. As much as I loved the baby I was carrying, the three of you were just as important to me, and I wouldn't give you up for anything."

"Did you tell him who it was?"

"No. Not for a long time. I don't know when I told him. I might not have told him until years later. But I couldn't afford to leave my children. I had such wonderful things with that sweet macho man. He was a *mensch*. He had his dreams of me just as I had my dreams of him. He would pick me up and carry me and put me in his bed. It was a different life, it was a different *man,* a different world—a very romantic romance, maybe too much. But it was good. He made me feel good, made me feel like a woman. Not just like someone who's hired to take care of the children and fuck him when he felt like being fucked. And that's all Daddy ever made me feel like. A maid."

I must say, I never saw one instance of my father treating my mother like a maid. He wouldn't have dared. But that is not to say that she couldn't have legitimately felt like a maid in relation to him.

"Why did the affair with Benno end?"

"Because Daddy said it was impossible, and I had to tell Benno it was impossible, because he would take the children away from me, and that was that. I had to stop seeing him. When I got pregnant with Joannie, Al went to a lawyer and said he was going to take the other three children away from me, he said I could have Joan since he knew it wasn't his. I couldn't let him do that, because as much as I loved Joan, I loved the three of you too. It's like if I have four fingers, I'm not going to let anyone chop them off. I'm certainly not going to let him chop three of them off and keep one of them. So I gave in. He had me over a barrel. There was no way that I could get out of it. I was stuck."

"It still seems strange to me that if the two of you were in love with each other, you wouldn't or couldn't find ways to continue seeing each other."

"Well, his mother went ahead and pressured him. And—he got married. She pressured him that he should get married, that he should not be hanging around with a married woman, which would lead nowhere, it wasn't fair, and she really did a number on him. He met this bookkeeper at his uncle's place, who at that time was making a lot of money—bookkeepers always make a lot of money—and he married her. He called me, he cried, and told me there was nothing he could do. They had got together and pressured him. And he felt it was the honorable thing to do."

"The only thing that's hard for me to understand—I'm sure you're right but—how could Father have gotten custody of all three children when he didn't take care of us much? If you had called his bluff, *he* would have been stuck, because he never would have been able to take care of us."

"He would have found a way. Even if he'd put you in an orphanage, he would have found a way. All he had to do was prove to a judge that I was an unfit mother, and he would have proven it simply by virtue of my having had an affair. Then he started saying he was going to jump in front of a train. And you know he did jump off of a dock one time, to kill himself, and was fished out of the water. He used to blackmail me: every time he tried something different. I would get further and further into this quicksand, and there was no way out."

"Why didn't Benno and you run away together with the four kids?"

"He had a job, he had to work. He was only a workingman; he wasn't a millionaire. He couldn't have afforded to pay for a divorce, or support four kids and a woman and move somewhere. He used to dream that he could. But what good would it do? Dreams are wonderful, until you face the economics. You have to be realistic, and you do the best you can. When Joan was born, he saw her, and he played with her. He used to throw her up in the air and catch her. He was a furrier: his stepfather Hymie was the one who brought me to the place where I bought my fur coat, my mouton, when I was pregnant with Joannie."

It's a novel. A whole novel, or a woman's picture, with the stars twinkling above and Ravel's *Bolero* playing in the background. When I read *Anna Karenina* and *Madame Bovary* as a teenager, it didn't take much for me to transpose these narratives into my family's story, my father being poor Karenin, whom I always felt sorry for, or Charles Bovary, the most sympathetic character in the novel, while Emma Bovary is running off with her dashing lover Rudolph, who would ditch her in the end. It seemed obvious to me that my mother was fooling herself, there was never any chance of Benno staying with her. I once saw a photograph of this Benno, he looked like a lifeguard grinning in the water. I half-imagine him to be always submerged in water, a Neptune with a trident. The fact that his English was halting, especially in comparison to my father's enormous vocabulary, must have made my mother feel comfortably on an equal or superior footing in relation to him. A Socialist, that part is admirable. Upton Sinclair was not the best of writers, though *The Jungle* has a clumsy power. And then he goes and marries a bookkeeper. Well, what's wrong with a bookkeeper? But it certainly cuts down on his romantic allure. I like the way she puts the blame on Benno's mother for doing "a number on him," no doubt with a German accent, like Claude Rains's mom in *Notorious.* My brother Lenny still remembers with chagrin being lugged along by my mother as a cover for one of these trysts, and having to wait downstairs. That ugly aspect, my mother didn't talk about. She had fixed all the other details in her mind, I'm sure having gone over them for decades, down to the consoling mouton coat, which became a second skin for her, and the pee in the snow. That brilliant naturalist fiction touch.

As for my father, the irony is that not only was he not prejudiced against this fourth child, but he actually showed more affection to Joan than he had to his own biological children. It may have been that by this time he'd developed a greater ease around small children, or because Joan was so sweet-tempered herself that he could only reciprocate in kind. In any case, it was not in my father's constitution to be unfair to a small being by holding her parentage against her. I doubt he entirely forgave my mother, but he took on the responsibility of caring for this fourth child without missing a beat.

## *File Clerk*

When my mother was in the hospital giving birth to Joan, we were taken care of by a rather sweet African American babysitter. As soon as my mother was able to get back on her feet, she hired a series of caretakers—some more lazy and incompetent than others, but none disastrous—to watch us children, while she found employment. She went back to work as a salesgirl at Hearn's Department Store. "Until one day my feet said to me: 'No. Enough is enough. Go get yourself a job as a file clerk.' I know my alphabet; I know how to file. I got a job as a file clerk at a company called Radio Receptor. After two weeks, the main office asked for someone to do other kinds of clerking work. So they sent me because they thought I was very bright. I worked as a clerk doing other things for about two months, and I managed to be appointed supervisor. It became a way of life with me. I would start out low man, and work my way up till it became too much for me to handle—either I would quit, or sort of be asked to quit. And then I'd start again, at the bottom. It never took me long to become a supervisor.

"At Radio Receptor, I had to send the government quotes for spare parts. I was aghast, because I would be quoting parts for seven hundred dollars or eight hundred dollars that I was buying for seventy or eighty cents. I said: 'How can we do this?' Even then, that corrupt business with military contracts was going on. They were giving me reasons like, 'By the time we finish processing, with the bookkeeping and paying your salary and general overhead, it's going to cost us eight hundred dollars.'

"During that time I had weird things happen to me. In Williamsburg there was a man who would make up personalized wooden photo albums. I walked into his store to order a photo album, and I said, 'Good morning,' and he said, 'Good morning,' and he reached over the counter and pulled me forward and gave me such a smooch. I said to myself while he was kissing me, 'No one would believe this.' I wasn't the most gorgeous creature that ever lived, but . . . Anyway, I got out of Radio Receptor and took a job at Lewitt's. That's where I met Willy." [We will get to him in due time.]

## *My Mother's Body*

My mother had a large body, veering between plump and quite overweight. When I was a young boy she seemed to me enormous, but she wasn't that tall, about five feet five inches. She had shapely legs, though her thighs bulged and were covered with purple varicose veins, probably the result of four pregnancies and standing on her feet a lot. I would stare at those varicose veins involuntarily, remembering her warnings about getting lead poisoning if you were jabbed by a pencil: the blue line might travel to your heart and you'd be dead. Rather like a snakebite. I imagined those varicose veins traveling up her legs to her groin. She often went around in slips, so there was no way of avoiding her corporeality. I found my mother's overly abundant flesh distasteful. Though I grew up a firm believer in Freud's Oedipus complex, it puzzled me that I never found my own mother physically attractive. Was I secretly wanting to sleep with her and overcompensating by concentrating on those elements that would repel me? I only know that when I read novels or memoirs in which the main character declares that he had a very pretty mother, I find it exotic, and wonder what other complexes I might have had if that had been the case. As it was, I always seemed to want to get away from my mother when she pressed me against her enormous bosom; I had to hold my breath to escape the slightly sour milk smell combined with talcum powder.

Dominant mass culture, even back in the 1940s and 1950s, taught us that only the thin and comely had the right to romantic sexual happiness. But here I was at an early age, eight or nine, confronted with the anomaly of this large woman, to whom I owed everything, ruled by her desires for love outside the marriage. It was a useful lesson to absorb that everyone has needs and desires, regardless of body type. I also wonder if proving her sexual attractiveness by taking lovers was not only a revenge against my father but also a response to her own children's disbelief in her physical desirability. This bizarre, monomaniacal notion, as though I were somehow responsible for my mother's adulteries, probably stems in part from my sense of guilt for rejecting her by wriggling out of her embrace. She would respond by blocking the door whenever I started to leave, demanding a kiss as her toll. Of course children are notorious for refusing to see their parents as sexual beings. They may experience grownups in general as monstrously gross in comparison to their delicate selves. Orwell put it this way: "People are too ready to forget the child's *physical* shrinking from the adult. The enormous size of grownups, their ungainly, rigid bodies, their coarse, wrinkled skin, their great relaxed eyelids, their yellow teeth, and the whiffs of musty clothes and beer and sweat and tobacco that disengage from them at every moment!" Even as a boy I felt pity for my mother, trapped as she was in an overly fleshy container. I could appreciate that she had a pretty face and a vivacity that pulled people towards her. But all her life she battled her weight.

"What was food to you?" I hear myself opening the subject on the tape.

"Anything that fit in my mouth. I had no preferences. I liked Italian food, I liked Jewish food, I liked Greek food. Give me chicken, give me steak, give me chocolate.

"Let's get back to the candy store. I used to live on ice cream and Coke. I used to make myself shakes. I'm surprised I didn't have a gall bladder attack from that alone. That was my whole diet. And I smoked constantly. I put on a lot of weight at this time. Then I started to get hooked on amphetamines. I would take the weight off, I would put it on again, then I would take it off. I started on amphetamines when Betty Ann was a baby. I saw myself in the photographs looking heavy and I was so young. Everyone was taking amphetamines; they didn't know what the result was. Dr. Diamond started giving me these different-colored pills, to take in the morning, the afternoon, the evening, and at four o'clock in the morning I would be ready to go out the window. I had no idea what it was doing to me; I never came down. I was up, way up there, all the time. When I started to come down, then it was murder, because it does terrible things to your disposition. I guess you people must have suffered through it. If I suffered through it, you kids must have suffered through it. I was always irritable. At work, anything anybody said to me, I was hypersensitive: 'Don't talk to me in the morning . . .'"

"Or in the afternoon, or at night."

"Exactly. We had a little television set. I wasn't terribly interested in it. I used to sit in the bedroom and read. The television set was in the kitchen. And you kids used to sit on the floor and watch. Daddy would say: 'Don't you want to come out and watch?'—'Leave me alone!'—'Don't you want to sit in the bosom of your family?'—'Drop dead! I don't want to be bosomed! I don't want any family!' I didn't want to be bothered; I didn't want to be touched. I had the feeling that my skin was raw, like it had been rubbed by steel wool. I didn't really feel good until I could eat something. But I was afraid to eat, because I knew I was going to put weight on again."

I do remember quite clearly my mother coming home from work and shouting as soon as she walked in the door, "Why isn't this place cleaned up? I'm supposed to do everything around here?" and sweeping all the plates and glasses off the table with one arm motion. It was something to see. We could barely suppress giggles at this flamboyant display of rage. I had no idea then that her crashing from amphetamines was the cause of these outbursts, I simply assumed there were people in the world who blew their stacks, like my mother, and others, more phlegmatic types like myself, whose place it was to watch the spectacle without commentary. Years later, when my mother went into show business, I would watch her onstage and think back to these fireworks as preparation for her theatrical performances. Too bad they'd been wasted on us; she needed a properly numerous audience.

"You never had hallucinations from the speed? It just made you energetic and then cranky?"

"I went through the hallucinations, for a very short time, when you guys were in high school. What put a stop to it was when Betty Ann said: 'Oh, Jesus. Mother's an amphetamine head.' And I realized that that's what it was. Because I wouldn't take the pill in the afternoon, I would take just the one in the morning, and I would be down at night, so grouchy, Jesus! I mean, don't even pass my way! Don't even breathe on me! And when I realized what was happening to me, I stopped it myself. I said I'm either going to fight it myself, or I'll be fat. So I'll be fat. Anyway, you can't stay on amphetamines for years, or you'll wind up in a straitjacket. I'd stay on it for a few weeks, a few months, lose weight, and get to a point where I'd be crazy. And stop. And then hope that the weight would stay down for enough time so that I could try to get into the habit of not eating. But unfortunately, you don't really get into the habit of not eating, because when you have to cook for a family . . . Then I tried analysis, I tried therapy. That doesn't work for the problem."

"Didn't you ever come to the conclusion: 'Eh, that's my body. Accept it.'"

"I got to that a short time ago. But then Dr. Grossman started in on me by telling me if I'm going to keep on being this heavy, I'm going to die. According to Betty Ann, I'm self-destructive. You see what I'm doing now? I don't keep anything in the house to eat. I won't permit Daddy to bring anything into the house. If he brings home something sweet, I stick it in the freezer. If he brings home bread, I stick it in the freezer."

"Did you go on binges, or was it noshes, or—"

"Yes."

"Everything?"

"Yes! [laughs] Whatever. The only reason I was not bulimic was that I didn't throw up."

"When you were eating, what did you experience? What was the existential meaning of eating for you?"

"The big problem with my weight has been eating at night. Usually I'd get up during commercials, go in the refrigerator, grab a piece of bread and butter, and eat. I wasn't necessarily hungry, but I'd look for food. I'd ask myself, what am I trying to gratify? So I'd start thinking all the way back. When did I start eating for gratification? I didn't start getting up at night to sneak into the kitchen until I was about twelve years old. It was only after my parents died. I was looking for the one thing I didn't get from whoever was taking care of me or living with me. I was looking for the love I didn't get. Since last week I'm not eating at night. Besides, I don't want to die—yet."

## *My Mother the Political Activist*

Frances had placed us in The First Hebrew Day Nursery, a childcare facility that I remember in retrospect as being benign and tranquil. That is to say, I was left alone to do finger painting, and to climb on the monkey bars in the playground, and to practice my seductive arts on the teacher. This nursery was across the street from a yeshiva, and I used to watch the kids with their long forelocks and skullcaps and droopy pants playing punch ball in their schoolyard, amazed that they could circle the bases in much the same way we secular kids did. The street that separated the two institutions had been the scene of several traffic accidents in which children were run over. My mother decided to get involved, along with several other mothers she knew.

"We went to a PTA meeting one time, and we said: 'We know that one of the kids from the yeshiva got killed by a car. That street is not protected by a light. We think there should be a light there.' They told us: 'You should talk to Mr. Sharkey about it'—he was the city councilman for that district. We said, 'Okay, if it isn't done by the next PTA meeting, would it be all right if we decided to do something about it?' They said, 'You go and speak to him first.' So we went to Mr. Sharkey to ask for a traffic light. We didn't even get to see him. We went to the Mayor. We didn't get to see him. We didn't get to see anybody. So we sent a note into Mr. Sharkey, and told him we had tried to see him, and if we don't get the light by such-and-such a day, we were going to have a baby carriage chain across the street. We never heard anything from him. So Tuesday night, I got up at the meeting, and I said: 'The last time I was here, you told us to speak to Mr. Sharkey, we tried to and nothing came of it. Tomorrow we're going to have a baby carriage chain. Who would like to join us?'—'Oh no, no, you mustn't, you can't block the way!'—'Why? One kid got killed, another one got hit by a car, it's not safe. My kid has to cross that street. So don't tell me I had better not.' That was the worst thing you could say to me. Nobody says to Frances Lopate, 'You had better not.' The meeting was over; there was screaming and hollering. I said I gotta go home. At one o'clock in the morning our phone rings. Mr. Sharkey is on the phone. 'You had better not.' Arrrgh! You just said the wrong thing to me. I said: 'Had you read my note, had you taken the trouble to see us when we visited, you would have known that we meant business.'

"The next day we wheeled out that carriage chain. Daddy had gotten a roll of paper from his factory. He had rolled it from the kitchen into the living room, and we had painted on it: WE WANT A TRAFFIC LIGHT. We hung it across the street. Somewhere I have a picture of the policeman tearing it up, and another picture of my friend Gloria on her knees scotch-taping it together. Somebody called *The Daily News,* they came and took pictures, and we got the traffic light! You see, that to me is important. I'm a fighter, but not always. If it's just for myself, like fighting Daddy for a divorce, then, no. In this situation, I had a whole bunch of people behind me."

"I seem to remember that some of the mothers on your side were Communists, and they were trying to capitalize on this local incident as a way to organize."

"No, we made fun of the Communists. Just the idea of them was funny. The American Communists were spouting a party line that could never work in this country. They were just talking into the wind. I will say, I signed petitions about the Korean War that I was advised not to sign. I didn't care—what could they do to me? But the Rosenberg case, that shocked me. Because at that time, it was already after the Second World War, I had gotten over the candy store exhaustion. I had become more aware of the world, and less preoccupied with myself in that negative way. I already had Joan, so I already knew there was something out there that could make me feel better about myself. I knew that somewhere there was a man, it didn't have to be Benno anymore, that there were some people who could make me feel I was a human being. I was no longer going to be a floor mat, a dishrag, unless I wanted to be. So I was ready to look at the world. I was out of my isolation ward. And I was really shocked at the Rosenberg case. I signed petitions. They should not have been put to death. Because there were so many spies that were being arrested and thrown into jail. So you give them a year or two until you find out for sure. To put them through that, to put those families through that, it was wrong, absolutely wrong."

"Did you think they were not guilty?"

"I wasn't sure, but even if they were, it didn't matter, they should not have been electrocuted. You don't put them to death. This was supposed to be a better country. The hysteria through the whole McCarthy era, that's when I woke up. I opened my eyes and I said: 'There's something wrong going on here. I may not be involved in it personally, but I *am* involved because it's my country.' First of all, you couldn't take what the Communists said seriously, that's why I thought McCarthy was so dumb. He was taking this shit seriously! They were no more able to overthrow the government at that time, or at any time, than I was."

"You were becoming a bit of an activist with that traffic light business."

"Yeah, I was getting involved with Gloria and Dotty Bader, but that didn't mean I was a professional activist. I was an activist when it made sense to me. I wasn't an activist for the Party. I was an activist for that traffic light because I saw kids being hit by cars. To me, children crossing that street had to be protected. It had nothing to do with democracy, Communism, or anything else. Essentially, I'm apolitical. I'm just a good person. I'm a saint." [She laughs incredulously.]

"Do you remember the sarcastic skit, when you made fun of the principal?"

"Oh, that! That was marvelous. Gloria wrote it and I acted it. We made Mrs. Unger look so ridiculous. She *was* ridiculous, picking on mothers. When one mother let her kid pee in a chamber pot by the bed instead of waking her up in the ice-cold night and walking her to the bathroom, Mrs. Unger didn't want to admit the kid to the nursery school. One time she was complaining because a kid had a very smelly bowel movement, and she wanted to kick him out of the center. I mean, kids stink, let's face it! She was a martinet."

## *Gloria*

When my mother first moved to Williamsburg, she suddenly found herself alone and friendless, in sharp contrast to her previous candy store experience, where she had known and got along with everyone. My sense is that in the old Queens neighborhood she had been more popular with the males who hung around the candy store than the females, but in Williamsburg she started befriending women who sent their children to the nursery school. They would babysit each other's kids when one of them had a job or an appointment. She went to a mahjong-playing group once a week. Her closest friend was Gloria, an intelligent, sharp-tongued woman with a sardonic sense of humor. They hit it off right from the start. Gloria was a chubby woman with glasses and a fish-face, and hairs on her chin, who had trained to be a nurse before marrying her husband, Jack. He had been in medical school when his mother got very sick, so he dropped out to take care of the family business, a candy store [another candy store!].

"What did you like about Gloria?"

"She had a fast mind, and that crazy wit of hers. She would come out with the weirdest things, and I would pick it right up and go along with it. That's what she liked about me. They were going to build a causeway from Miami to Havana, and she said: 'But you can't build a causeway over a deviated septum.' And I said: 'I know. When we get to that, we're going to dig a tunnel.' She used to have this routine that would drive me crazy. We had a bell, but I didn't want to have to go down the two flights of stairs, so I'd call 'Who is it?' and she'd say 'I'm looking for that woman Elaine whose husband just got out of jail.' She'd stand there on the street saying these outrageous things, until I'd put the key in a bag and throw it out the window. Finally I had a key made for her."

"Let me ask you something. How true is the rumor that Gloria had lesbian designs on you?"

"I don't know. I have a feeling that it's something she fought very, very hard. It's very possible. She always wanted to sleep in my bed. She kept her hands off, that I'll admit, but she always wanted to sleep on my side of the bed. And she used to hug my pillow. She always wanted to wear my clothes. She used to wear my girdle. She was terribly allergic to penicillin, and one time I had just had a penicillin shot on my butt, because I had a sore throat. She put my girdle on, and she broke out in a rash the size of lily pads all over her body. She might have had something to do with a woman at one time. Over the years there were conversations, little hints."

"But she never made a pass at you?"

"No—nothing overtly."

"She didn't like Father, is that right?"

"They were both jealous of each other. They used to fight over me. He was jealous of her because he felt she had too much of my time, and she was jealous of him because she had to go home and I stayed with him. Even as recently as the last time he was in the hospital, seven or eight years ago, she came to visit him and I was gentle to him in the hospital, and she said 'I gotta get out of here, you're making me ill.'"

"She really wanted you to be hard on him all the time?"

"Yes. But he was sick. There comes a time when you gotta be a *little* gentle."

"We didn't like Gloria when we were kids."

"Yeah, I know, you didn't like her being around all the time."

"She was so fixated on you that she never really became a member of the family."

"Strangely enough, the first time I broke up with Gloria was over Willy. She couldn't countenance my having an affair with a man, with another man. She never said anything, but she would find everything to discourage me. She just couldn't see it. It wouldn't have made any difference if he was Prince Charming himself with gold and diamonds dripping off of him, it bothered her terribly. In all my stupidity, even *I* started to suspect something: she was getting too possessive. I had to admit, it was flattering. Everyone wanted to get into Gloria's inner circle. She was the one who held a salon at her house that everyone wanted to go to. And I was the chosen one. She used to lock her arm into mine and say, 'We're engaged.' People used to look at us very strangely. After a while I started to feel like Dorothy Stratton, singing, 'Let me go, let me go, let me go, lover.'"

As for me, I came to like Gloria. She was the closest thing we had in our lives to an intellectual, besides my father. She would turn up for years after at family gatherings, asking me and my siblings with curiosity what we were up to. A stabilizing force. I don't even think she was that hostile to my father in later years: when she nearly gagged at my mother treating him gently, I think it had mostly to do with her doctrinaire opposition to any display of sentiment, which she equated with sentimentality (as did my mother, often).

## *Willy*

After my mother left Radio Receptor, she got a job at Lewitt, a company that manufactured vacuum cleaners and also spare parts for the troops in Korea. "I did highly specialized work in Lewitt. I put stamps on machinery, and I was very good at it. Not very intelligent but very good." It was there she met Willy, a coworker, and embarked on an affair with him. I was eight at the time, and remembered it forever after as an explosive situation that almost tore the family apart. My mother wanted to leave the marriage and go off with Willy to California, taking the kids with her. It seemed at the time that my younger sisters were willing, but my brother and I held firmly to my father's side. I did so largely at the coaching of Lenny, which in retrospect seems odd, since he was always fighting with my father. Normally sympathetic to my mother, I was torn between affection for her and loyalty to the men in the family. My father tried every means to keep her from leaving: he wrote a series of love poems to her, he begged her, he threatened to take the kids away from her, and (in my memory at least) he gave her a beating. All these events I eventually put in a story called "Willy," which took me ten years to write, so traumatic was it for me to recall that chapter of my childhood. Yet in our taped interview I was struck by the breezy, insouciant way my mother spoke about the episode. One person's trauma is another's footnote.

"Willy was light black, very light. You didn't realize that he was black at all. He was a ladies' man, a real charmer, and a lot of fun. He would do things that were unexpected. I once went to the movies with the girls, and when we came home, I was getting the key in the door and there he was parked out in front. I didn't expect him to be in Brooklyn—he was sitting there waiting for me. He was nice, he was sincere, and he liked you kids. He was a good man. I—I didn't love him. I didn't have the same feeling for him that I had for Benno, but I could have. If it wasn't for the fact that Daddy got hold of me at that time and talked me blue in the face, got hold of him and talked *him* blue in the face, I could have probably been happy with Willy. I don't know how long it would have lasted, probably not that long, but he would have been a way out of the marriage, which was a bad situation."

"I didn't know Daddy talked to him."

"Yeah, he did. He walked him down to the docks, and after it was all over Willy came and said to me, 'I didn't know what the fuck that man was talking about. He just talked and talked and talked and talked. How can you stand it? All he did was talk.'"

I suppose Willy expected the proper response for a husband whose wife he was sleeping with was to bop him in the head, and then he could have fought back.

"The gist of it was that Al would never give me a divorce. If I started a divorce action he would fight it. I had no fight left in me by that time. After that, any man that I had anything to do with, it was no longer a relationship, it was a purely sexual thing."

"Remember my story 'Willy'? Was it true that Father left the house and checked into a Y?"

"Yeah, he did. But he came back, because he said he couldn't afford to eat out three meals a day, and because your father needed a maid."

"Why did he leave in the first place?"

"I guess his pride."

"And he was writing you those poems at the time?"

"Yeah. Full of big words, showing off. I had to use the dictionary to read them. Big deal. I laughed off all his threats. When I came home one evening, late, seeing him standing at the head of the stairs, I swear to God, it was like one of those cartoons of the wife at the head of the stairs with a rolling pin in her hand, waiting for the husband to come home. It sure was funny at the moment. He was so angry at me at one time that he took all my earrings and my necklaces and broke them up in little pieces. It's a good thing I don't wear expensive jewelry."

"I remember Father beating you, towards the end of your time with Willy."

"He never beat me. *Never* beat me. If he ever raised his hand to me—he did try to choke me to death. I woke up one morning and found his hands around my throat. He tried to kill me that time. He also tried to knock me down a flight of stairs on the subway, but he will deny it to his dying day."

"Can you ever remember him laying a hand on you?"

"If he tried to beat me, he would have been on the floor. He might push, but he never hit. Because he knew better than to hit. You might have thought he was hitting but he never hit. He hit Lenny. But he never hit me."

"Well I remember both of you hit us a lot when we were growing up."

"It warped you? [laughs] My poor baby! It stunted your development?"

"I could have done without being beaten, to be very honest."

"I guess I couldn't. I guess I needed for you to be beaten." [she laughs]

"Well, that's a good answer. You never felt guilty for using an ironing cord on us?"

"I used to threaten with the ironing cord more than I hit you with it. I think it was raised around my head more than it landed on your legs. I don't say that I didn't hit you; I know I did. But I had to. I'm not a psychiatrist. I remember going into the house of a psychologist in Williamsburg. We were in the kitchen, and his two children were in the living room, and they took some building blocks into the living room, their uncarpeted living room, and started hammering on the floor. He asked them eventually, not right away, to stop. The reason why he asked them to stop was because he said the people downstairs were not 'emotionally ready' for banging over their heads. Now, evidently I was not that psychologically tuned in, I didn't have the degree in psychology that would allow me to say: 'No dear, you mustn't do this—'"

"You're making it sound ridiculous, like there's no other alternative between hitting children and letting them stomp all over you."

"Of course, there's a halfway. But I didn't know then. I told you at the beginning: I had no role model."

"But your parents didn't beat you."

"My sisters beat the shit out of me! Don't forget, I was a real battered child. You weren't. You got hit and got spanked, but I was battered after my parents died. The fact that I hit you as little as I did meant that I must have used considerable control, compared to what was done to me."

"I always thought that by the time Joan came along, you didn't hit her nearly as much, like you had a change of heart."

"Because I'd learnt from experience, from reading and going to lectures that there were other ways. Unfortunately, I didn't have that background when I started childrearing. You people suffered from it. I guess it didn't harm you *too* much."

"I'm not saying it warped me, I'm just saying that there was a certain amount of brutality in the household, and some of it was between you and Father, and some of it between the parents and the kids. There was an atmosphere of violence—maybe not that frequent, but it occurred. Father had a very strong hand and you had an ironing cord."

Despite my attempt to guilt my mother about hitting us in the interview, I have to say that it seemed no big deal at the time. Better a slap on the tush than to hear long lectures about "disappointing" one's liberal parents. I also regarded beatings as part of our world; in the street or the marketplace, I would see working-class parents hauling off and smacking their kids without hesitation. My parents were an odd mixture of working class, by virtue of their factory jobs, and middle class, by background. Hence, they settled into the murk of the lower middle class, splitting the difference.

"So, getting back to Willy . . ."

"Joannie was already in nursery school, that's why I got fired from Lewitt. We worked on the tenth floor, and I couldn't get to the clock to punch my card and go down the stairs and get to the nursery school to pick Joannie up in time. I would punch Willy's time card out, so that he could drive me to the nursery school. But they caught me punching his card, and they fired both of us. Anyway, I had gotten pregnant from Willy. I had no intention of having this guy's baby—"

Perhaps her knowing he was slightly black had something to do with that; maybe not. "He was married too, wasn't he?"

"He was married. I found out he was married and he had another woman, another mistress. I said: 'You're a sweetheart, you're a darling, you're wonderful and I love you and everything else, but it's much too complicated.'"

"He wasn't really going to go off to California with you, was he?"

"He *would've,* if I had stuck to it. But he wanted to take his daughter with us too. He said: 'You don't want to leave your kids? I don't want to leave mine either.' And I didn't blame him. But I decided to have an abortion, and I contacted this woman. Remember the nurse who came to the house? She sent you out for Kent cigarettes."

"I just remember there was a lot of screaming in the bathroom—"

"That's right, I had gone through an abortion, and it didn't take. Part of it came out on the kitchen floor, like a piece of liver."

"And then you threw it down the toilet?"

"What else was I gonna do? Put it in the crib?"

Both of us laugh: such is my family's black humor.

"The second time the abortion took," she adds.

"You seemed to have bad luck with the carelessness of your lovers and contraception!"

"The funny thing is that the last lover I had, no matter what, he would never ejaculate inside. Even after I had had my hysterectomy. It didn't make any difference, he just had to go where it didn't do anything."

TMI.

## *My Father's Poems*

I keep an envelope in my file cabinet of my father's poems. They are immensely moving to me. We're not talking Thomas Hardy or Cavafy here, only an amateur poet, but still, they exhibit a decent attempt to press feeling into form. Here is one he wrote after the breakup with Willy:

Pyrrhic Victory

You bade farewell to your lover
And returned to my waiting arms.
My patience had brought victory.
What is victory?—merely a word,
An empty term, a delusion.
Your body was fused with mine
But your mind and heart were aloof.
I touched you, pressed and
Ardently caressed you. All this
Left not the slightest imprint
On your coldly forbidding self.
How can I recapture the bliss,
The thrill of exciting yesterdays?
Will time ease the pain and
Restore a really true contentment?
Or must I evermore nurse a gnawing
Suspicion, a growing fear that you
Will once again leave me? And
I will have to start my endless vigil.

It's curious that my mother, a sensitive, intelligent woman, would not have been touched by this effort to win back her love through poetry. Perhaps she was simply too far gone in her anger against him to do more than snort at his memories of "bliss," or she was put off by the tone of reproach that kept seeping into these appeals.

I had occasion as a boy to see him pen one of his poems. Sitting silently beside him, watching him cross out phrases, move lines around, or pause to find the right word, had an incalculable effect on me and on my choice of vocation. I could have been a boy raised in the circus, gazing up in wonder at his dad as he walked the tightrope.

My becoming a writer would also explain identifying more with him than with my mother and her lover, who scoffed at his trying to resolve the situation with language. "I didn't know what the fuck that man was talking about," Willy had said. In her preference for the linguistically challenged Willy over my father, I can't help feeling her sexually rejecting—me, or the type of man I am. She freely admitted that Willy was not as bright as my father, but insisted that intelligence isn't everything. He was "nice," he was "fun." He was also married, and had a second mistress on the side—in a word, trouble. My mother may have been drawn to him for that very reason, as a fellow "sinner," or let's say, one with a different moral compass, who saw nothing wrong with extramarital affairs. It surprised me to learn she did not think their affair would have lasted much longer than a year, and that she was only looking to him as an expedient way of leaving the marriage. Apparently she didn't imagine she could start a new life, simply leave my father, without a man alongside pledging his love. But again, as with Benno, she was likely fooling herself that he would have thrown over his whole life just to be with her.

I wonder if my insistently identifying with my father around the question of adultery, this willingness to feel self-pity for the cuckolded male sex, is a way of masking my own waywardness. After all, there were certainly times in the past when I slept with someone I wasn't supposed to, or let my dick dictate over my brain. To the degree I followed my mother's example of affiliating with Eros, avidly wanting to *live* and satisfy carnal appetites, I should identify with her at least as much as with my lugubrious, depressed, fearful of being left, Thanatopsis-inclined father.

## *My Father's Chief Regret*

The same summer I interviewed my mother for twenty hours, I also did a taped interview with my father, which lasted only an hour. That was about all the words I could squeeze out of him. By this time he was seventy-four and rather addled, so I don't know how much I can trust his testimony. Still, there were startling admissions, like the following:

"Let's get to the nitty-gritty. When we were first married, your mother was unfaithful to me. And I found out. And one day, I found myself choking her. In the middle of it I stopped short. Because I said to myself: 'Why am I doing this? This is not me. I am not a violent person. I am not a person of action.' Then I stopped, and that's when your mother had me. Because she had something she could always hold against me."

"Why didn't you leave her then?"

"That's the story of my failure, because I just couldn't leave her. I'm not saying this in defense of myself; I said that I made a mistake. If I could have killed her, it would have ended then and there. I would have been tried, sent to prison or executed, and that was that. This way I let everything linger on and solved nothing."

My father's greatest regret was that he didn't kill my mother. As with her confiding her amorous adventures to me, he thought nothing of the effect this statement might have on me, as her son. The mind reels. Still, why protect me from his inner reality, which went a long way toward uncovering what lay behind his perpetual silence?

"And that would have been the only way to solve the situation?" I asked him.

"I don't know if it was the only way, but it was a solution. What ensued was not."

"How would you characterize what ensued?"

"Years of nothing, of humdrum existence."

It seems then that they were in accord in this judgment that their marriage to each other was hell, robbing their lives of happiness and meaning. This hatred my parents had for each other, up to and just short of homicide, was like Strindberg's *Dance of Death*; I must take my hat off to them for their depth of passion, dark as it was. I am made of blander stuff. Still, what puzzles me is why, if my father felt the situation was intolerable, he didn't simply pick up and leave. Or why she couldn't leave. Her excuse was that he would have tried to take the children away. I doubt that she couldn't have found a workable separation somehow, if she had wanted to enough; and as for him, it couldn't have been fear of losing his children that kept him matrimonially chained, since he never seemed that attached to us. Was it simply something about the culture at the time, the rarity of divorce? No, that couldn't be it; they stayed married long after divorce had become commonplace. Maybe their mutual hostility was what they had gotten used to: the devil you know is better than the devil you don't know, that sort of thing. My wife Cheryl posits that there was more love between them than they could acknowledge, and it was that which kept them together. Then again, she tends toward looking on the generous side of things.

## *Singing Lessons*

My mother had a sweet, pretty voice, which was surprisingly thin considering what a large woman she was. She could not belt out a number like Ethel Merman, but she could put it across, as much by acting skill as by vocal projection. She was a natural comedienne, and even when she sang a torch song, there was a hint of comic discordance, a touch of irony, which she played up onstage, as if to say: "I guess you didn't realize a big overweight mama like me could have such tender romantic yearnings."

"I wanted to ask about your getting interested in singing. Were you taking lessons at that time?"

"I did take singing lessons when we were living in Williamsburg. I went to a teacher, an Italian man named Joe Presti. He lived in Brooklyn, some residential part you had to take a long bus ride to get to. He was in his thirties, fairly young, just short of medium height, brown curly hair, and a pleasant Italian face. He had a good baritone voice of his own, and he used to sing opera, those operatic duets like the one from *La Traviata*. He told me a very interesting thing—that some of the greatest voices are never heard because of stage fright. Anyway, I did musical shows for the First Hebrew Day Nursery. I sang for them and it was fun. I never ever wanted to give up singing. I always sang as a kid. I was the chosen one. I stood on the kitchen table when I was three years old and sang and danced. In the back of my mind, I knew that someday I was going to go on the stage. Someday you children were going to be old enough, and I was going to be able to walk away from all this. And sing."

"So what kind of training did Joe Presti give you?"

"Classical. He was bringing the mezzo up. But he didn't do it for me. Unfortunately, as a man he couldn't explain the sensation that I was supposed to have when I was singing. The only teacher I've had that really did wonders, that could really get my voice back in shape, was Stephanie, because being a woman she knows exactly what I'm supposed to feel. But Joe tried. At least he made me understand that my voice *could* get bigger, could get better, and I wasn't using it fully. I was doing light classical songs like 'Oh, Promise Me,' 'I Love You Truly,' that sort of stuff with him. I couldn't do opera; it was too difficult. I was doing Helen Morgan torch songs. I remember when I began singing 'Summertime' and I found it so hard to start off on that high note, and Joannie said, 'You mean like this?' She sailed into that high note, and I said, 'Oh my God, if they worked on that girl's voice, she could be some singer.' What was she—four, five years old? But they told me that I shouldn't force a child that small; it would ruin her vocal chords. And later on, she didn't want it; she wasn't interested."

"Did Joe Presti tell you that you had talent?"

"He told me I didn't. He told me I could have, but I didn't know what to do with it, and he said I'm not worth working on. On the one hand he encouraged me, and on the other hand, discouraged me. But he encouraged me enough so that his discouragement didn't work. It gave me the feeling that if I had a better teacher, I could do better—I didn't need him."

"How did you learn to play the piano?"

"The same way everyone learns: you take lessons. I got that old beat-up piano, and I found a piano teacher that somebody recommended. She was a Mexican, she didn't speak three words of English. She used to make me keep the beat—'No, no, no!' I liked my own phrasing, my own timing. I didn't want to play it the way it's written. She said: 'But that the way it's written on the paper.' I learned a little bit. But what crossed me up was the scales. I got so bored with the scales. That happens with almost everyone who takes up the piano: You get bored with the scales and you stop."

It's interesting that she objected to having to keep a steady beat. My brother and I, both jazz and blues enthusiasts in our teens, started playing Billie Holiday records in the house, and my mother, who had already taken voice lessons, would carp that Lady Day was singing behind the beat or hitting the note flat or sharp, not understanding that was the whole point. She was competitive with Billie Holiday, God love her.

## *Other Flings*

As I was interviewing my mother, a name from the past popped into my head: Victor R. Greenblatt. He was a friend of my parents—or my mother, I should say—and an insurance agent for Metropolitan Life. We visited him on a few occasions in his comfortable Ozone Park home. He spoke with pompous elocution and a flowery vocabulary, like certain rabbis of the old school, and he seemed quite full of himself.

"How did you come to know Victor R. Greenblatt?" I asked, unable to keep a tinge of irony out of my voice. (We kids always mocked the man behind his back, as much for his insistence on using a middle initial as for his orotund delivery.)

"Victor was our insurance man. When we took over the candy store, we got to know him and his wife Elsie. He was brilliant, in his way. He wouldn't play bridge with us because he thought he was too good for us. After a while we said, 'Okay, let it be like you say.' But we used to socialize with them a lot. Outside of the Lopate family, he was the most pedantic person I've ever known. One night he argued the pronunciation of the word *precedent* until dawn. That was the sort of relationship we had: intellectual, purely intellectual. Until, as happened with a lot of our friends, he started coming onto me. I could handle him—I could always handle them."

"You never had an affair with Victor R. Greenblatt?"

[Pause] "Not till many years later. Not till we lived in Brooklyn. Then I had him going crazy. He used to ride the elevated train in front of our apartment on Broadway, back and forth and back and forth, and wait to see if the curtain was up. If the curtain was up, that meant that he could come in, no one else was home. I would sit in my house and pray that he would go back home and stop bothering me. He would call and he would cry and kvetch and beg. If there's anything I cannot stand, it's a man who begs. That turns me off. If you're disappointed, you're disappointed, but don't beg. No woman is worth begging for."

"No man, either."

"Well, I never begged. But no one is worth crying over. Anyway, eventually they moved away."

"That was before your affair with Willy, or after?"

"That was after, because by that time, I was pretty soured on everything. I got so angry with Daddy that I was ready to accept Victor. I started to feel—abandoned. I started to feel that I was ready to *act* with abandon. You get the picture? But I found he just wasn't for me. I . . . I can't understand men. Do men really feel that they're God's gift to women? That no matter how often a woman says no, they don't really mean it? That they're so terrific that a woman really wants them?"

"They're just listening to their own needs. I don't think men think they're so terrific."

"But men never take no for an answer."

"Sure they do."

"Unfortunately, the men I knew and had dealings with could not take no for an answer. Unless—I've been thinking a lot about that—unless there was something in me that, although I would tell them no, it's like the song lyric goes: 'Your lips tell me no, no, but there's yes, yes in your eyes.' It's very possible I'd send out a mixed signal, because I had a great need for—but I was afraid of that need, it scared me silly. It frightened the devil out of me."

"What was the need for?"

"It was just a need for affection. And I found that when you encourage a man to be affectionate, immediately he takes that as a signal to be sexual. A man can't put his arm around you and hug you and hold you and stroke your hair without immediately getting an erection and wanting to have sex. I couldn't deal with it. Because I didn't want sex, I wanted love. And I didn't necessarily want passionate love, I just wanted affection. I wanted someone to tell me I was nice. I didn't want someone to treat me like a doormat or a servant. I wanted to be treated *nice*. And unfortunately, men don't understand that. They see it as a come-on, like, 'Woops, let's hop into bed!'"

"I have to defend my sex. I have platonic friends. There are plenty of friendships between men and women who show affection to each other, but they don't go to bed together."

"Well, unfortunately I didn't find any like that."

"Maybe because they knew how unhappy you were—"

"And I suppose they also knew that I did need sex. I did. Oh boy! I mean, when a husband comes right away, premature ejaculation, even premature premature. . . . I went through a period when I didn't have lovers. I was completely frustrated. I wanted a lot of lovers but I didn't have that many. There were—I'm not going to start making lists. That would be of no particular advantage to either one of us. I will say that my brother-in-law Morris came over one time and tried to go to bed with me, and what stopped that was the fact that I laughed at him."

Dear Uncle Morris: he, of the Groucho Marx resemblance, a lawyer in good standing with the Democratic Club, who always gave the impression of sneering at everyone, most especially his chirrupy wife, Aunt Gladys, and being above it all. This came as a shock. Now I would have to picture him chasing my mother around the bedroom in his boxer shorts. "So you never slept with Morris?"

"Just once. *Just* once. He had to see a client one time at Kings County Hospital, when we were living on Brooklyn Avenue. And after we went to bed, I laughed at him. That stopped it."

"Why did you laugh at him?"

"Because at the time I had a lover who was such a fantastic sex machine, Herbie, and here this mutt comes over and I just had to get rid of him, and the only way I could get rid of him was to do it. By that time I was smart enough to know that sometimes you just gotta, in order to get rid of them. Which I did. When my sister Gladys used to complain, 'Look Ma no hands,' I knew now what she meant. So after he was finished I laughed at him. Which I think is the worst thing you can do to any man."

Wow. She was betraying her sister and expressing her disdain for the male sex all in one fell swoop. At the same time, I admire her worldly, Wife of Bath carnality and practicality: how to get rid of an importunate suitor.

## *Therapy*

Around the time we were living in Williamsburg, my mother started going to see a therapist. She had developed some sort of stomach problem, with frequent attacks of diarrhea, and would throw up till blood came. Our family physician, Dr. Diamond, sent her to a clinic in Manhattan, and they diagnosed colitis, which at the time was thought to have a psychosomatic component. They advised her to see a shrink. She eventually took their advice.

During the early 1950s, Freud was a name to reckon with in Jewish Brooklyn, and even though my family lived in the ghetto, barely scraping by financially, with one foot in the working class where therapy hadn't yet made significant inroads, my mother was willing to be a pioneer. Between singing lessons and psychotherapy, she seemed to be reaching for answers.

My mother had come to her therapist on the recommendation of her friend Alan Kolber, a photographer who later went into business partnership with her. The Kolbers, Alan and Dotty, were the only couple friends my isolationist parents had at the time. They would hang out in our messy apartment in Williamsburg, seemingly oblivious to the disorder. I would also babysit their brats from time to time. They were staunch believers in psychotherapy. Alan had even written a memoir under the influence of sodium pentathol about his unhappy childhood, entitled *The Key to the Cage*. He was, come to think of it, the first author of a book (albeit self-published) I ever encountered.

"The Kolbers had come into my life through the nursery school. They were very important in my life. Because of Dotty Kolber, strangely enough, I learnt an important lesson about my sister Dorothy. See, Dotty Kolber was always available for emergency babysitting, just as I was for her. Many times she would ring the bell, and there she'd be standing with her kids, Michael and Shelley. She'd say she had to work, and could I bring them to the nursery? Of course I could. My kids were there already, why not? I'd sit them down, give them breakfast, keep them busy. If I needed emergency babysitting, *she* was there. One time my sister Dorothy was complaining to me—[her son] Robert was a baby, about a year older than Joan, I think—that she had something to go to and she couldn't find anyone to babysit. No problem, I said: I'll come over from Brooklyn, I'll babysit. She said, 'No, I don't want you to do me any favors. Because if you do me a favor, you're going to want me to do you a favor and I don't want to do any favors for you.'—Aha! Okay. I knew then exactly where I stood with my sister Dorothy. That closed the door on our relationship. We were no longer sisters; we were acquaintances."

[Naturally, any story my mother told had to take a detour into the wrongs her siblings did her before it could get to the main point. However, the vignette does illuminate a sharp contrast between the warm, communal mutual support among working-class mothers in our poor neighborhood, on the one hand, and the hardhearted selfishness of more well-off women like my Aunt Dorothy, on the other.]

"Well, Alan found an analyst, Dr. Jonas. He was a Viennese psychiatrist who had an office in the Bronx. He taught Alan how to hypnotize himself. The only problem with hypnotizing himself was that when Alan worked in a toy store over Christmas one time, and he was selling a loop-de-loop toy, he watched the thing and all of a sudden he went out. He hypnotized himself and couldn't come back! Alan was a loser. That was why he was undergoing analysis. Anyway, I decided I wanted to see Dr. Jonas too. So I went. He would charge me five dollars an hour. He was the first one to tell me I was being provoked into misbehavior, that my husband needed therapy more than I did. He wanted to see Daddy, not me. He said, 'There's nothing wrong with you. I have to see your husband.'"

For the most part, during these interviews I kept my mouth shut and let my mother chatter on, telling it her way. Every once in a while I would throw her a curve ball. This was one of those times;

I could not let her statement pass without commentary. I was also curious to see how much she might acknowledge the point I was making or ignore it. In any case, it seemed to me too far-fetched that she was enlisting this therapist to say she didn't have any emotional problems, they were all on my father's side.

"But that wasn't true that there was nothing wrong with you."

"But your father was provoking me into the kind of behavior that was giving me these terrible guilt feelings."

"Oh, sure. But don't you think that you had enough emotional problems stemming from your past that you could have benefited from real therapy?"

"What I was going for was what I was being provoked into doing, like being unfaithful to my husband, or wanting to leave him. Here was this 'paragon of virtue' who never left the house, didn't drink, didn't gamble, didn't run around with other women—I wanted to get that problem out of the way first, because the marriage was what was bothering me. I wanted to know why am I behaving in this way, why am I having affairs? Why did I spend a weekend away with Willy? Why am I doing all this, when this man is so perfect? And so, Daddy went to see him. The doctor told me there's nothing he can do for Mr. Lopate, the man's a brick wall. He was the first one to tell me that, but not the last. . . . I went back to Dr. Jonas and I learned a few things. I don't remember what. He lived near Moshulu Parkway. I remember going down this very steep hill to him in the winter, and I fell. I couldn't get up again, because of the ice and snow. There was nothing to hold onto. I thought I was going to have to spend the rest of the winter on Moshulu Parkway."

"Were you ever in group therapy?"

"I went into group with Dr. Jonas when he moved to Park Avenue, in the East 70s or 80s. He moved his family into Westchester, and took a suite in this very classy brownstone. Group therapy was a problem, because the only time Daddy would babysit for me was Friday night. He did not like to babysit with you kids. And Saturday, which was the day when the wives would go to group, he refused. He flatly refused. What was I supposed to do? So I said,

'All right, I'll go on Friday night.' But they were all guys, and practically all of them had mother problems. There I was—Mama. Their attitude was: 'Who knows what this woman sitting there is doing to her sons?' [We both laugh] 'Who knows how she is fucking up their lives?' I'd sit there and they would talk and talk. Me, never said a word. Can you imagine me in a group, never speaking? Then they would point to me and say, 'Look at her sitting over there with that smug, supercilious expression on her face.' I wanted to say, 'You fucking bastards, I'm not your mother, what do you want from me?' But the angrier they would get, the quieter I would get. That made it even worse. If they would ask me something directly, I would speak very quietly, very refined, like a schoolteacher. That would drive them up the fucking wall! I was so contained, and the doctor tried *everything* to break me down. He tried everything to make me cry. He said I wasn't gaining anything by the group experience. I was still in individual therapy. We all were. But even alone with him I couldn't talk."

"Why do you think that is?" I asked, sounding like a shrink myself.

"I don't know why. I would lie there and not talk. It got so that he'd pick up the phone and make appointments: he would call his bookie, he'd talk to his stockbroker, he'd take care of everything else. I could not talk to him. He didn't urge. See, that's the reason why I was able to get along with Mike, who I started seeing recently—"

"But it's a different kind of therapy. In psychoanalysis the doctor is not supposed to guide the conversation. That's the whole premise of psychoanalysis: free association as directed by the patient."

"But I did much better with Mike, because he asked me questions. I made more progress with Mike."

"Who else was seeing Dr. Jonas? Weren't there some famous writers or actors?"

"Rod Steiger was in the Friday night group. He was still married to Sally Gracie. And one time she came on Friday night because the Saturday when her group was supposed to meet was a holiday. Joseph Wiseman, the actor, was his patient too."

"I have a theory," I said, ever on the lookout for explanations having to do with class, "that part of what was intimidating you was that the whole experience was not only teaching you a new vocabulary but introducing you to another socioeconomic group."

"No, none of those guys were so well-off. One of them worked for the post office. He used to sit on the floor and say in his thick Brooklyn accent, 'I know that I could never attract girls until I know that the feeling is mutual.' They were a strange cross-section of people. One was an actor, one was a stockbroker, one the post office clerk, and there was Alan Kolber, who was no bargain. Anyway, after a while I didn't feel I was doing anything with Dr. Jonas. To be solitary and quiet and stew in my own juice, I didn't have to pay *him*, or make that trip into the city. The only time I talked—the one time he made me cry—was when he gave me sodium pentathol. He injected it into my veins, gave me a big yellow pad of legal paper and a couple of pencils, put me in an anteroom, and said, 'Here, write.' I didn't think I had anything to write. I wound up writing and writing. One of the things he latched onto was that my brother George—now this was under sodium pentathol, it isn't something I made up, it had to be the truth—used to take me up to the attic and fondle me. I could never understand why I hated my brother George. I didn't remember any of that. It didn't bubble up to the surface until that day."

"How old were you when he fondled you?"

"About four. He was about fifteen years old. I'm surprised he didn't rape me. I think the only reason why he didn't was that he was afraid I'd tell. He would take my pants down and touch and feel and poke—and now he's got that holier-than-thou attitude, he's so fucking sanctimonious."

"And you sent *me* off to his house?"

"By that time he was too old to do anything. And you were only ten years old."

"You were only four years old!"

"Yeah, but you could kick him in the balls if he got too close."

My dear Uncle George: he reminded me of the comic actor Ed Wynn, with his bald oval head and glasses. He was a successful architect who lived with his wife and children in Brookline, Massachusetts. One summer my mother sent me off to Uncle George and Aunt Frances, to get me out of our sweltering Brooklyn slum and give me a taste of middle-class life, maybe even polish my rough edges. George had recently suffered a heart attack, so I was told not to bother him, not to put any strain on him with childish demands. I didn't. He was in any event not particularly fond of children, and was once heard to say at a family gathering that we little ones should "go play in traffic." I have no idea at all whether there was any truth to my mother's recovered memory of having been abused by her older brother. It would certainly explain some of her ambivalence towards men; but then again, she could have arrived at the same mistrust through other paths.

## *Changing Residences and Jobs*

We moved from the wretched tenement at 352 Broadway, facing the elevated train, to quieter, more pleasant digs on Ross Street—still in Williamsburg, but more upscale residential. It was so middle-class, in fact, that we didn't fit in. "We moved there because I felt it was time for something better. I have always wanted to better my living conditions. I was working. I wanted new furniture. I wanted a nice living room. Lenny was going to have his bar mitzvah soon, and I wanted to be close enough to the shul, to the public school—things like that."

My mother had gone into business with her photographer friend Alan Kolber. Together they formed Kewpie Studios, which specialized in child photos. "Alan Kolber was a fabulous photographer. He photographed a little black baby against a backdrop, and he lit it up, and the kid looked like he had a halo, like an absolute angel. I would set up appointments: I was doing what's called 'kidnapping'; they were infants just home from the hospital. They couldn't be brought to the studio. We used to get them when they were two weeks old, these tiny little bitsy things that could barely hold their heads up. He would make gorgeous pictures of them. Unfortunately, he didn't have enough money to buy a car, and he had all this heavy equipment. Alan Kolber was a five-by-nothing, maybe he weighted one hundred fifteen pounds soaking wet, and he was carrying a piece of equipment that weighed as much as he did, and he couldn't do it. And I, with my salesmanship, was making one appointment after the other."

"Why didn't you go out with him and help him carry some of that stuff?"

"I was making appointments. He was taking the photos, and I was working the telephone. That was the way we had set it up. It was really a good business, or would have been if he had had a car. He used to schlep the stuff by train, by bus, until he pulled a muscle in his leg and in his back."

My mother would sometimes go into the coat closet to make her phone calls, separating herself from any noise we kids might make. She had developed a smooth sales pitch with a honeyed voice, different from her ordinary mom one: we thought it utterly phony and would ridicule her tone, though she was doing the canvassing mostly for our sakes. Meanwhile, she was running up astronomic phone bills, and the house was growing messier by the day.

Here I should reiterate that my mother was an indifferent housekeeper. Why mince words? A slob. Her natural tendency was towards proliferation. The landlady at Ross Street would look in on us from time to time, while we kids were running around half-naked, unsupervised. "The landlady was going to dispossess us because the place got so dirty and the cockroaches ran all over the place. Ooo! she saw one cockroach and freaked out," my mother said disdainfully.

It was more than one roach; it was mayhem. The landlady brought two policemen to witness the mess, they took pictures, and the next thing we knew, my parents were summoned to court; the judge upbraided them and gave us thirty days to vacate.

We moved next to Washington Avenue, on the border between Fort Greene and Bedford-Stuyvesant, at the time an almost all-black neighborhood. It was roomier than the place on Ross Street: one bedroom was shared by my brother and me, and another was occupied by my two sisters; my parents slept in the pullout couch in the living room. A further advantage was that the neighborhood was down-at-the-heels, the owner absentee, and no one would evict us for being slobs.

"Did it bother you that we were living in a black neighborhood?"

"No. Not at the beginning. Not for a while. Not until I came home and found Lenny's blood dripping all over the lobby and the elevator, then I knew I had to get out of there."

"I remember he was beaten up badly by a tough kid named Pete. He had a way of not knowing how to back away from a fight."

"I was never frightened of black people. And the funny thing is, one time I was living on Brooklyn Avenue, and I was walking from the subway home, and as I was crossing the street I was saying to myself, 'Isn't it a shame that people when they see a bunch of black kids, they get so scared and they cross the street.' And as I'm saying that these fucking little kids come up behind me and grab my purse and run. [laughs]

"As far as moving into a black neighborhood, that was the only place we could afford. When we were thrown out of Ross Street, I moved into Washington Avenue because it was a clean building on a clean street. I went to the apartment during the day, there were no kids around. There were no people on the street. I didn't know it was a black neighborhood! In Ross Street the Hasidim used to throw garbage out of the window. Here the streets were swept, the building was kept clean. There was no such thing as graffiti at that time. The black super, Mack, was terrific. And Mrs. Danziger—she was Mack's girlfriend—sat there and she always looked like she had just come out of a shower. She always looked so pink and clean, with the cigarette smoke coming out of her nose. Her hair was always pulled back and always looked damp, like her permanent had grown out and the bottom was all ringlets."

I was always astonished at my mother's physical descriptions of people: how vivid and precise they were. I remembered this Mrs. Danziger as slightly scary, half-sow, half-dragon, perpetually wreathed in cigarette smoke, leaning one beefy arm out the window and watching disapprovingly as I threw a rubber ball against the building's stone cornice.

My mother decided to open a photography store on Myrtle Avenue, adjacent to a public housing project. It was the candy store redux, except this time there was more involved than mixing an egg cream or making a malted.

"Tell me about the photography store."

"After we moved to Washington Avenue, we rented the store. I got in a lot of equipment, I had a very nice little store there. The trouble is I didn't sell enough to be able to pay the rent and all the expenses. The neighborhood was just too poor to support a store like that."

"Did you start the store as an offshoot of Alan Kolber's photography?"

"No. Kewpie Studios was already finished. It's just that through him I got to know Amvet—the place that was developing the films. I bought a lot of the cameras from them on consignment, and others I bought outright."

"But you didn't know that much about photography. How come you started a business you knew so little about?"

"I had been a salesgirl in department stores. Selling a camera was no different to me than selling a man's shirt. I didn't sell expensive, complicated cameras. I knew how to load a simple camera. At that time, nobody was going in for those 35mm cameras. I didn't carry that kind of camera. I sold the film for it, but I couldn't load it. I also had paint-by-number sets, little gifts. I had a film developing service, where you bring in a roll and come back for it the next day. Nothing complicated."

"Was Father working there at the store?"

"Occasionally on weekends. When we decided to close the store, I paid all the debts. I figured no dealer who sold something to me in good faith should have to swallow the loss. I don't believe in going into bankruptcy for a thing like that. Actually, I took a loan, and Arthur cosigned it. I paid all the debts, got a job, and paid Arthur back. That was the end of it. That was a quickie. Anyway, I really tried. I wanted us to have our own business. See, I tried everything to get Daddy away from the factory, Parkside, because I knew that Arthur was taking advantage of him. And he was putting Arthur first before everyone. Just think, if Arthur hadn't said no, Al might have been a general in the Israeli Army by now. I wanted to go to Israel. At the time when Israel became a state, and they wanted young people to go into the kibbutzim, I didn't know that there was a fund set up for people like us with young children, where we could have gotten there free. But Arthur said, 'No, you can't go, because I won't help you and give you ten thousand dollars.' All we wanted was ten thousand dollars. I didn't know about these other funds."

My father the Israeli general. The road not taken. I can just see him with an eye patch, like Moshe Dayan, leading the tanks through the desert.

"Why did Arthur say no? He needed Father to work for him?"

"Because he had a perfect patsy there, who devoted his life to Parkside. And when everybody got raises and he didn't get a raise, because he was too loyal to join the union, Arthur gave him 'gratuities' from his own pocket. Now the gratuities meant that Daddy got the extra ten dollars a week, but Arthur was able to take that off his income tax. Also it meant that Daddy got cheated on all those years of Social Security that were not paid in. So Arthur never did Daddy any favors. I tried every which way to get him out of Parkside. The only way he was able to get out of Parkside eventually was that Parkside went out of business.

"I remember what happened. Some friend of Arthur's, some schmuck named Fred wanted Pop to invest in a yarn dyeing business. So Arthur staked him to it. Now Daddy's idea was right: when you're building a business, you take a small salary, pay your employees, otherwise you're going to lose them, pay your debts, and later you can take the big salary. Well, his partners didn't want to do that. They wanted the big salary first and the hell with everything else. Daddy didn't like that. So he sold out. They bought him out. He gave Arthur back his money. By that time Parkside had closed. Daddy had had a chance to buy Parkside with his dyer, who is the most important person in that business. They couldn't get the money together to finance it, and Arthur was never too fast with the buck."

"Why couldn't Arthur give Father a deal on the sale of Parkside?"

"You're asking the right one. You're asking the one who was told, 'Be nice to Arthur and Doris, because they can do more for you than you can do for them.'"

"Let me ask you a question: In all those years you were trying to get Father out of Parkside, what if he really wanted to work at Parkside?"

"He felt comfortable there. But he did well once he got out of Parkside—"

"Yeah, I know that you wanted him out of Parkside because he was giving everything to the job, but supposing that he liked the job?"

"But they were misusing him, they were abusing him," said my mother.

"Maybe he wanted to be used. Maybe he felt comfortable there and maybe that's who he really was. You couldn't accept it but—"

"I begged him at least to try to take courses to better himself, so we wouldn't have to live in these shitholes. Nothing. He wouldn't do anything to better himself, so long as he had Arthur. You see, Arthur was his God. I didn't feel it was fitting for a grownup man to have a *putz* like that for a God. Have a *mensch* for a God!"

"But I know what it's like with a younger brother looking up to an older brother. Anyway, the Gods that people seek are always withholding. That's what makes them Gods. If Arthur had been forthcoming all the time, Father could have overcome his adoration."

There was no sense in pressing the point.

## *Herbie*

When the photography store went out of business, my mother took a series of jobs in the garment center, then the largest employer in New York. She would start at the bottom of the pecking order, get a few promotions, then leave out of boredom, until she settled at M. Lowenstein & Sons, one of the nation's largest textile companies.

"I was in my late thirties, almost forty. It was 1957. It was just after New Year's. I went to Lowenstein and I took their test, and I came out very high. I got the job, with a little bit more salary than they had advertised. I think it was forty-five dollars a week, instead of forty. Or seventy-five dollars a week. Fifty-five dollars a week? Some ridiculously low salary. They sent me across the street to Pacific Mills, which they had just bought. 1407 Broadway, that's where I started to work. I would take a bill of lading and enter the case numbers, the bale numbers, and how many yards were in there and how much it weighed and how much the whole thing cost. I was keeping some kind of record of shipments. I took to office work like a duck to water. As much as I hated all kinds of arithmetic in school, I think that I was meant to be a bookkeeper, because I really enjoyed it. To make a column of figures come out even or five figures of columns come out right was a tremendous victory. I loved it. I even enjoyed the bump on my finger—I had never had one before.

"So the job was okay, but my Pacific Mills coworkers resented anything to do with their new owners. I would get into an elevator with these people who hated the fact that they were now Lowenstein employees, who would look through me at each other, and say, 'So many new people here.' I was the only one there. I would stand there and laugh. Of course it hurt. I wasn't there for friendship, I could have lived without them as friends. . . . A Chinese kid would come in, looking for some invoice to Burlington, and they would say, 'Boy, every type works for Lowenstein.' And the secretary said, 'No, he works for Burlington.' 'Oh.' But if he was Jewish, forget it. It was 'the Jew company this, the Jew company that.' It was starting to get to me. You see, Pacific Mills was an anti-Semitic company. That's why it was so surprising that Herbie worked there, but they didn't know he was Jewish. His last name sounded German. He didn't look Jewish at all. He was blond, with a round face.

"After M. Lowenstein bought Pacific, they put up glass partitions instead of making little offices. The offices became an open bullpen, which really bothered me, because there was no privacy. I hated that. I wanted it to be quiet: when I was busy, don't bother me. I didn't want to have to look up and see from across the room somebody's got their eye on me. And that's what would happen. I'd look up, and there would be Herbert watching me. I saw his eyes bore right through me. He always smiled, very polite. Never came on. But I felt his presence—he was there, watching me all the time.

"Then I moved across the street to Lowenstein. Herbie stayed at Pacific. Everything was better for him because then he was able to make his approaches by telephone. He would have me meet him at very classy restaurants. Jesus, I had lost all that weight, and I really looked terrific. I walked along the street like I had a broomstick stuck up my ass, great-looking behind, spiked heels on, all the eyes used to pop out of their heads. Cheap dress: I never spent a lot of money on my clothes, but whatever I wore looked good on me. And I'd get one rose off of a vendor, or one carnation, swinging a rose—oh, did I know what I looked like! And—he couldn't help it. So we started making afternoon liaisons. I would take the day off. I never took a sick day when I was sick; I used to take a day off when I felt good. Because when I was sick I used to come in and work; I didn't care how bad I felt. He would take out his appointment book: that was really strange, I'd be fitted between two appointments.

"By that time we had moved to the high-rise building in Flatbush. He used to wait in the lobby where we lived until Betty Ann left to go to school, and then he'd come up the elevator. When he had a meeting at night with the Knights of Pythias, Knights of Columbus, some sort of organization, we used to meet in the Piccadilly Hotel, or one of those places around 42nd Street, but it was still a nice hotel, I don't remember which one. He'd always call me, tell me he'd rented a room. And I would just meet him after work. I'd go right up to the room. He'd already signed up at the meeting, and we'd spend a whole lovely evening in his hotel room. He'd usually have dinner for me. We'd have something from a classy delicatessen midtown, Wolf's. He had a little half-refrigerator where he kept soda and stuff there. And we'd have a feast. Once a month, we had our meeting there, and once or twice a month, he would come to me in Brooklyn.

"The man was a wonderful sex machine. He knew just what was going to turn me on, he knew when it was going to happen, and he did it terrifically. But it was like going for a sauna. You worked up a good sweat, you got up, you dried yourself off, and you'd go home. Anyway, Herbie was quite a mechanic. He knew what was going to make me jump, really jump. And then we had nothing to say to each other. He had no conversation. He was an absolute dyed-in-the-wool Republican. We couldn't even argue politics, because we gave it up as a lost cause. He couldn't see my point of view, and I couldn't see his point of view. We were on opposite sides of the fence. He had a beautiful big home, he was making a lot of money, he had two kids, everything he ever wanted. But he had a very sick wife. She had had numerous operations on her back, and she couldn't stand any pressure. She had all his love and his devotion and his loyalty; but he was a man with appetites. And I was a woman who had—not much of a husband, and I had appetites. It was a terrible blow to me when Herbie died. I was devastated, because he was the only link to my physical side. I didn't need him for anything else. He had no connection to the intellectual—he was not like Benno. Benno was an intellectual, he had the physical thing, youth, he was fun, running up and down, he was for everything. But Herbert was strictly for one thing. And I needed him for that one thing. When he was gone, there was nobody else to take his place. . . . I remember I showed you a story I'd written about a woman whose lover dies, she's devastated, and you didn't like the story, you wrote a very nasty letter back."

Here I must take a moment to comment on my mother's writing. She would write short stories about a sensitive woman (herself, obviously) surrounded by clods and nincompoops who could not appreciate her sensitivity. The stories were heavy-handed, mawkish, and a chore to get through; I would try to balance praise for whatever worked (that old writing workshop dodge) with a dollop of advice about how to make it better, which she would ignore while taking deep offense that I did not consider it perfect.

An aside: One of my first short stories, written in high school, was about a woman my mother's age who dreams of getting contact lenses to improve her looks, and finally saves up enough money to buy them; then one of the lenses falls down the sink as she is trying to insert it. This actually happened to my mother, who was the model for my story, an unconscious appropriation of Gogol's "The Overcoat" with contact lenses taking the place of the coat. I was channeling my mother's self-pity. My English teacher, Mr. Fenner, returned it with a comment that I was "squeezing the banana too much," meaning: being manipulatively mawkish. His just response struck me with considerable force, and I began to develop a more resolutely unsentimental way of writing, steering clear—perhaps to a fault—of pathos.

But my mother's short stories were drenched in pathos. I note as a curious fact that they had none of the juicy vivacity her conversational storytelling did. I love her description of walking down the street with all eyes on her. Suddenly I see my mother in a 1930s Warner Brothers movie, one of those Barbara Stanwyck Pre-Code vehicles where she plays a working girl who knows how to use her assets and sleeps her way to the top. Then it turns into a Yiddish movie, with the two feasting on pastrami, corned beef, and sour pickles, maybe even Dr. Brown's Cream Soda, from a *good* delicatessen, a classy one like Wolf's on West 57th Street. Not like the one where she had her wedding reception.

"I don't remember it as being such a nasty letter, just unenthusiastic," I said. "It was hard for me to read a story about you and your lover. It was hard for us as your children to accept the fact that—hard for me, I'll speak for myself—your having lovers wasn't merely a youthful error, that this was something you were determined to pursue. I didn't realize at that time how—how trapped you were. I naturally felt that—"

"That I was a bad wife, I was a runaround, I was a tramp. [sighs] Yeah."

"Those were the images we were fed from movies, and it was more or less the way I was taught to think. And then when my first wife cheated on me, I felt the pain of it doubly."

"You can't dwell on that. You have to keep it locked up in a little cubicle in your mind."

"No, I don't dwell on that. It's just that some betrayals cut deeper. Well, how did Father react to these men? Was he aware of Victor or Herbie or any of the others after Willy?"

"I don't think he was aware. I never told him about it. I'm sure he knew that something wasn't kosher. But look, after I realized that this whole thing was not going to be the ideal, made-in-heaven marriage, when I first got the courage to act, I was not the most tactful person in the world. If I could be hurt, I was going to hurt back. And I really could be hurt!"

"No doubt. But I think what was hard for us as children to see was how *you* were hurt, because you were so much more visibly the attacker, and the way that Father hurt you was so much quieter, often we just didn't see it. It seemed like he wasn't doing much."

"You realize that the quietness was what he was doing to hurt me. His silence alone, the fact that he was not acknowledging that I was alive . . ."

"I didn't take that as a personal affront, because that was what he did to all of us. You would get angry at him—obviously, you had expectations of him that were much greater than we did—but all I saw was that he had treated you exactly the same as he treated all of us. He was silent to all of us. Of course you were his wife, you had a right to expect more, but to me he wasn't doing anything out of the ordinary, and suddenly you got angry at him. [She laughs] That's the way it looked to me, and it still looks that way sometimes. I come here and I watch you flare up at him, and I think, 'Well, Pop is just being Pop. What's the difference between the way he was fifteen minutes ago and now?'"

"Or the way he was fifteen years ago and now? True. He wasn't any different then than he is now."

## *Father's Plunge*

"Could you tell something about that period when Father tried to kill himself? What that was all about?"

"Well, I think it was about money. Lenny had been going to a fancy college, Pratt, and his scholarship didn't cover the whole thing. Even though I was working, and Al was working, he was not making an awful lot. It just was not enough. We didn't think it was fair for Lenny to be going to this expensive school when he could have gone to Brooklyn College. It wouldn't have killed him to go to a city college. But was it really just the money? Al felt like such a failure. And here I was going blithely along my way, doing my own thing and getting promoted. They put me in a production job that only men were doing at Lowenstein; I was one of the first women to do it."

"So you weren't doing so badly. Was the family in real financial trouble?"

"We were not in financial trouble if we didn't go overboard and go into debt."

"Did he think that if he killed himself we could get the insurance?"

"Probably." Clearly she is either bored or reluctant to engage this subject. Her responses are becoming monosyllabic or reduced to one sentence.

"But is that true?"

"I have no idea. I never discussed it with him because I was so disgusted with him that I just didn't care."

"Didn't he jump in the river or something?"

"Sure. *Somebody* fished him out."

"And then what happened?"

"He came home!"

"And you didn't ask him why he did that?"

"No."

"You weren't curious?"

"I didn't care."

"You know, I remember it so differently. I remember that you were very frantic that day."

"I was frantic, yes, that he didn't come home. He had never done that before. But when he did come home, soaking wet, and I found out he had jumped in the river, or the bay, off the dock or wherever it was, in Rockaway—"

"I thought it was in the East River."

"I don't know. I never found out where it was. Or if he told me, I don't remember. You know, it's like a child: you worry about him, and when he comes home, you don't care anymore, forget it. As long as he was home, I didn't care where he'd been or what he did; I was angrier that he put me through this. And I had reached a point in my anger that I wished he didn't come home at all."

"But that was the day you told Lenny about Joannie having a different father. And then Lenny couldn't take the pressure of keeping the secret so he told me."

"I don't remember anything about it. I don't remember the specifics."

"That's why I think you were more upset about it than you're now remembering."

"It could be."

"So . . . everything returned to the way it was, or . . . ?"

"Sure, everything returned to the way it was. It was the weekend. He got dried off and went to work. Why not? There was nothing dramatic the man could do, to get me to the point that I would sympathize with him or feel for him. There just wasn't. It's unfortunate."

"Wasn't it one of those times when you were building up to divorcing him?"

"Yeah, it was either that or the money. I think that was probably also a reason."

"So that wasn't powerful enough for you to give up your plan to leave him, right?"

"No, I don't think so. Had he jumped in front of a train, that's something else. But he kept on threatening. And I never knew what he was going to pull next."

She sounds so cold here, so unfeeling. Still, I've entertained the possibility that sometimes my mother was purposely putting herself in the worst possible light, exaggerating for the tape recorder, in order to make herself into a more theatrically colorful character. I wouldn't put it past her. In the scenario she had constructed of her life story, my father was the Minotaur blocking her path to happiness. She could confess everything, all her sins down to the most abhorrent thoughts: her one taboo would be admitting that she felt any tenderness, even love, God forbid, for her husband.

"What was Pop doing after the factory closed down?"

"He got a job in Lewitt. He joined the electrician's union. I was working at M. Lowenstein already, and going from one step to the other. I had started as a receptionist and worked myself up. But when he was working at Lewitt, there came a time to take an exam for an opening, and he got the highest mark and he couldn't get the job. Why they bothered to give an exam, I don't know. The union had already decided who was going to get the job. He was so disillusioned, so disappointed."

Shortly afterward, she badgered him, with the aid of her ex-lover, Victor R. Greenblatt, into taking the test to become an insurance salesman. He passed the written part, scoring high as expected, but flunked the oral interview section, which exposed his withdrawn nature. I am sure he was thoroughly relieved when he failed the test, but it was typical of my father that, rather than refuse from the start to have anything to do with this profession which so clearly ill-suited him, he went through the motions, letting passive resistance ensure the desirable negative result.

"Before that, Father was very pro-union, right—he wouldn't cross a picket line?"

"Absolutely. Me, I almost got killed crossing a picket line. When I was younger, my sister-in-law Hilda worked in some shop that was on strike, and she didn't care—she needed a job. She said to me: 'You want to work? Go scab a couple of days till the strike is over.' And I did. The strike was over and I was out of a job. But they got hold of the van I was in and they started rocking it back and forth. The cops came finally. I was scared. But it was very exciting, very exhilarating. I was ready to go back because it was so exhilarating. I think *that—that* is the thing with Pop throwing the tomatoes: no reason for it, just exhilaration.

"Let me digress again. The day my father died, I was nine years old. I was old enough to know something tragic was going on. I knew about death: when you're gone, you're gone. But everybody had come from out of town, all my brothers and sisters, I hadn't seen them in months, and in spite of the fact I knew something terrible was going on, I was so excited and so exhilarated. All those cars—wow! This ought to happen more often! Oh, that's terrible. The guilt!"

"No, no, it's natural."

"The adrenalin was running like crazy. All those cars."

## *Performing*

While she was working for M. Lowenstein & Sons, the textile company sponsored a musical revue in which its employees were invited to perform. This morale-booster, intended in the spirit of corporate picnics, Christmas parties, and softball games, strikes me as quaintly old-fashioned. In those days, too, the garment industry was located only a few short blocks from the theater district. *Pins and Needles,* a long-running musical, had begun as an International Ladies Garment Workers Union activity.

Lowenstein hired a talented pianist-songwriter named Bob Waxman to direct their shows. Waxman, who had come from a family of prosperous Atlantic City realtors, was in love with the American musical stage and eager to avoid working in his family's business. When he told them he wanted to pursue music, his father said, "All right, then you have to make your own living." He took in a few private students but found it difficult to make a go of it, so he accepted the job at Lowenstein. Bob Waxman was a portly, lively, highly emotional man in his thirties, flamboyantly gay, with wavy black hair, who looked like the actor Laird Cregar with maybe a touch of Raymond Burr. "I'm not a latent homosexual, I'm a *blatant* homosexual," he would proclaim.

"Anyway," my mother said, "there was a notice sent around: they wanted 'talent' for a show. I found out that every year they would do a show. I wasn't particular who I sang for. I figured what the hell, I can sing, I can dance, I can act, same as anybody else. So I tried out. I'll never forget when I walked into the cafeteria the first time and I saw him sitting at the piano, his back was to the cafeteria because the piano was up against the wall, and he was sitting there with his head in his hands, in profile. All you could see was that profile with the big sharp nose and the big blobby body and the black wavy hair. And the look on his face was unbelievable. It was, 'Oh God, what am I doing here?' Fine: I come in, I sit down, I don't know from nothing. I knew that I sang alto, because there was nobody else there who could carry an alto part without automatically slipping into soprano. He auditioned us, and it clicked. It was like when Gloria and I clicked, Bob and I clicked. And we became a real—couple. He and I hit it off just like, to use Gloria's crude expression: 'We fit like a finger in *tuckes*.'"

"Well, there were similarities between Bob and Gloria. They're both sarcastic."

"Oh, yes, yes, they were both bright, intelligent people, and I thirsted—I *died*—for people like that. Because when you work in an office with a bunch of lumps that only see the numbers in front of them, and the girls who think only about their date or the color of their fingernail polish, there comes a point where there's got to be some stimulation. And Bob and Gloria were both very acid, with a biting sense of humor. Bob would say something nasty about somebody; I would just pick up the ball and run with it. He knew he could depend on me to do that."

"I must say, I find it absolutely incredible that they hired a full-time person just to do a company show."

"Well, it wasn't exactly that way. You see, they also put him at a desk during the day with these half-assed orders and Bob would write little comments, draw flowers and pictures on them, and send them back to central filing. The supervisor of his department hated him, because the supervisor would pick his nose, and that's when Bob said to him, 'When it comes out, you should push it back it in, because it might be your eyeball.' I mean, how could you not fall in love with a man like that? When Bob needed rehearsal time, he would rehearse after five. But during the day, they had him at a desk."

"So did they paid him extra for the work after five?"

"Yes. But of course he took an awful lot of time off during the day to create—I mean, he wrote music and he had to write out scores. He wrote the song 'Just This Once' for me. I was afraid I couldn't sing it. He said, 'If you don't sing it, then no one else is going to sing it.' I had to sing it."

[In "Just This Once," a frumpy cleaning woman puts down her mop and fantasizes about all the pleasure in life she has been deprived of and would like to sample, just once, including "minks and chinchillas / a Spanish villa," ending with wanting to be "a well-kept woman / I'd like to play Scarlett, with Jelke as Rhett / Just this once.'" Mickey Jelke ran the biggest prostitution ring in the city, and was the tabloid sensation of the day. The song not only had clever lyrics but was uncannily suited to my mother, with her fantasies of romance and the high life.]

"I rehearsed and rehearsed with him, and then your father dropped the bombshell on me. I had suggested that he should go to see a therapist. As long as I was growing—and I felt at that time I was growing, I was getting promotions, I was getting raises, and I was starting to do things on the stage—he should see a therapist. So he went to a clinic that recommended a therapist for him and started going. Here I am, in the middle of all these rehearsals, doing these wonderful skits, and Lenny is working his little ass off doing the sets, and Al says his therapist suggests that I quit the show. Because I had suggested he look for another job, and thought maybe he would get a job with Victor as an insurance salesman. Victor would take him on, but he had to learn the spiel. So in order to learn the spiel, he had to rehearse it and make it sound natural, and the *ooooonly* one in the world he could rehearse it with was me. Albert had three teenage children at this point, old enough to listen to the spiel, who could help him with it. No, I was the *only* one, because his therapist said so. Of course I never checked it out by calling his therapist, and I don't think his therapist ever said that I should quit the show and sacrifice what I'm doing to help him learn his script. My attitude was: 'You're a big boy. You have to do it yourself. You have got to learn to stand on your own two feet. I cannot carry you.' So the result was, I refused to quit the show. See, again I was 'cruel and insensitive.' Forget what he did to me: I was always 'cruel and insensitive.'"

"Can I ask you a question? What possessed either of you to think that Father could be an insurance salesman? I can't think of a more unlikely insurance salesman."

"If he had a list of his own family and friends that he could sell insurance to, it would have been all right. He wouldn't have had to do much spieling. He could just go to them and say, 'Look, I gotta do this part-time—'"

"But you can't keep going just on friends and relatives as clients."

"You gotta try. You gotta try. I just wanted him to try *some*thing."

"I know, but he is so antisocial, how could he be put in a position where he had to sell something?"

"Well, the upshot was that he didn't do it."

"And my second question is: Did he know that Victor had been your lover?"

"No."

"In that sense, it was kind of strange to place him with Victor, no?"

"Victor would have done anything I asked him to. Anything at all. However . . . I did not quit the show. Not only didn't I quit the show, but on the in-between nights that we were not rehearsing, I took a part-time job working evenings at Macy's. So I would run like hell from work to Macy's, punch in, and whatever I earned, I spent immediately on clothing, underwear, shoes, all the necessities of life. He was complaining: 'You work and you work, I never see a dime out of it.' Of course, because I was spending it on necessities, like clothes, like shoes, like food. Anyway, he didn't get the job. He stayed where he was. He went in for an interview . . . You could never tell me that he tried. I know he didn't try. It's like when I sent him recently to apply for an apartment for himself, you can't tell me that he tried. Whenever he went for a job, his problem was that his desperation always showed. So much so that he never got the job. The more he didn't get the job, the more desperate he became, and the more he didn't get the job. That's the reason why I got him a job at Lowenstein."

"Wasn't there a period when he was out of work, and the family was literally in bad straits? I remember we were eating macaroni and cheese every night for a month."

"Not for very long. Yes, that was before I got a job. I was going from one supermarket to another to take advantage of their bargains. Fortunately the supermarkets were not very far from each other along Fulton Street. Sunday's big dinner was chicken fricassee, with the chopped meatballs and chicken wings. But it didn't last too long because I always managed to get a job. And he eventually went to work at Lowenstein."

"When you got that other job at Macy's, wasn't there something perverse about that? Here his therapist is telling you to help him, and you're saying, 'Not only am I not going to help you by quitting this show but I'm even going to fill up the rest of my evenings.'"

"Perhaps. But at the time I wasn't thinking that way. I was only thinking, 'Gotta make an extra buck.' And I'll tell you too, Dr. Diamond said to me, years before that, 'Either you're going to wind up in a straitjacket, or you've got to go out and get a job. I can't tell you to get on a plane and take a trip to California. But the further you get from your family, the better off you're going to be.'"

"Interesting. I told you I felt the same way at times." [A therapist I was seeing in 1980 told me: "Usually I try to get patients to confront their families, but in your case I would recommend putting several thousand miles between you and them." So I accepted a teaching post at the University of Houston.] "You felt it as well?"

"Yeah, but you could escape, I couldn't. The only way I could escape was to go to work."

"Didn't Father take a test to find out what his vocation should be?

"Yes, and they told him he would be very well suited for newspaper editing. But where is he going to get a job as a newspaper editor, out of the clear blue sky? He wanted very much to be a newspaper editor. He would have been fantastic."

"Why didn't he just take a job in a newspaper? He didn't have to be an editor immediately."

"When he took that test and went looking for a job, he did what I knew he would do. He went halfheartedly looking for a job. If he didn't get a job right away, he went right back like a homing pigeon to Arthur. And he was left with his frustrations and the knowledge that he could have done better in a newspaper. If he had started at the bottom, as a cub reporter—he had experience. If he had only given himself half a chance! But he wouldn't. He was so shy, so afraid to face new people."

"Okay, so he didn't get the insurance job and you went ahead and did the show. Which was correct: you certainly should have done that show."

"I'm not a person who is going to sacrifice my life more than once. I did it. I'd made that scene. I sacrificed my life once, maybe twice. I was not going to do it forever. I kept on performing, and then I got him a job at Lowenstein."

"What happened with the show on opening night?"

"Everyone was there. It was a real evening. I was very disappointed that Herbert wasn't there, but he hated Lowenstein, he hated the company, he hated the management. It's a shame, because I would have liked him to see how talented I was, how much fun it was. The whole cast and crew, we had such a close-knit relationship. After the first show ended, we went upstate to some place in the Catskills for the weekend. Youngs Gap Hotel, that was Lowenstein's gift to us. Lenny came with us. God, it was cold. We had a lovely time slogging through the snow, freezing our asses off. The whole group stayed together, and then we did a second show. They kept Bob on for that show, which was an operetta called *The Kiss*. We did that in the Joan of Arc Junior High School Theater. Betty Ann and Lenny painted the set, and it really looked like there were glass doors. Crazy, they were so talented! Betty Ann—where did all that genius of hers go to? I get sick over it."

"Weren't you also singing at that time at the Caedmon Memorial Church?"

"Sure, me and Betty Ann, we were singing every Sunday. Oh, that was fun, just getting out of the house every Sunday morning, and Thursday night rehearsals. I love to sing. I think I owe it all to some psychiatrist I went to who looked like Nosferatu. He would sit on the chair with those big staring eyes and a bald head and a long skinny nose, smoking one cigarette after the other. He had an ashtray piled up with cigarette butts. I was complaining that I want to sing, I want to sing! And he said: 'You want to sing? You really want to sing? Go places where there's singing.' I mean, how much more logical could you be? And that stopped me from complaining. The Orthodox Jewish choir wouldn't allow women in it, so I went over to the church."

"When you were in the church choir, did you feel any disloyalty to Judaism?"

"No, I was still going to shul during the High Holidays, but I had to sing. I took Betty Ann too to the church to sing. I guess maybe it is my fault that you people went away from Judaism."

"Why blame anybody? I had my chances, I was more exposed to Orthodox Jewish ritual than most people by the time I was thirteen years old. I was in a Hebrew choir; I had gone to Hebrew School for years."

"That's the problem—you were exposed to the Orthodox. Had I taken you to the Conservative or even the Reform temple—the Conservative approach is easier to swallow. That's where the resurgence is among young Jews today."

"So what did you and Betty Ann sing at the church?"

"We sang Handel and Bach, we sang 'Jesu, Joy of Man's Desiring.'"

"You were better off with Bach than the Hebrew repertoire."

"I sang the alto parts. I got along fine with them. I always got along well with the goyim. But I never became friends with the other singers outside the choir. I never tried. I was always working; I didn't have time to."

"At that time you seemed to be moving into a lot of subcultures different from the ones you grew up in, like the gay subculture, the black neighborhood, and the Lutheran church . . ."

"Why not?"

## *Betty Ann's Party*

Recently a friend asked me, "Which child was your mother's favorite?" I wasn't sure how to answer her, because it changed over the years. For a while I thought it was me: at least a neighbor told me so, based on her observations, when I was about thirteen, and I felt both pleased and guilty towards my siblings. Perhaps the burden of chosenness (if in fact it was even true) propelled me to start challenging her argumentatively, as I did with those teachers during that same period who singled me out for extravagant praise, thereby undermining them before they could incite my classmates' hostility.

She certainly doted on her oldest child, my brother Lenny, though with him, too, there would be rifts and complications. She always had a tender spot for her "baby," Joan, the youngest, not only because she was her beloved Benno's child but because Joan was so easy to get along with. Still, the one she was closest to, in her later years, was unarguably my sister Betty Ann. My sister would bring her laundry over to do at my mother's apartment house, and dine with her several times a week. It was not only a question of seeking maternal comfort but of being the most solicitously protective of my mother's health, especially after Betty Ann became a registered nurse.

"What was happening with us kids at the time you started performing? Were you worried about us? Did you sense us emerging as individuals in ways that surprised you?"

"I always worried about you. I worried about where you were, what you were doing. And I always blamed Daddy for my having to work. I blamed him because he didn't show enough ambition, he could have done better. Looking back at it, I see that it wasn't his fault. He *couldn't* do any better." [Interesting: she had just finished telling me she was happy to work two jobs at the same time because it got her out of the house and saved her sanity, and now she was blaming her husband for having to go to work because he didn't make enough money. I suppose there is a way of resolving this paradox, from her perspective.]

"You were part of a social class: you were lower-middle-class people struggling to keep your heads above water. There were millions in that situation. Why should you have been any different?" I hear my younger self ask.

In listening again to these tapes, I am embarrassed at the condescending, pedagogic tone I took at times with my mother whenever I tried to get her to see her situation in a larger socioeconomic context. Perhaps my motives were not entirely pedantic: I wanted her to feel less shame about her and my father's failure to reach what she regarded as their full potential. But in any case, she barely registered these remarks; they rolled off her back, while she seized on the one word (in this case, *different*) that would allow her to continue excoriating my father.

"Yes. We were two entirely different personalities. I was the kind of person who found that if I could do better, I *would* do better."

"But what I'm really asking is: Don't you think you were ascribing too much to a person's ability to take destiny in your own hands, and not enough to the forces that are arrayed against them?"

"I'm telling you I was the kind of person who could do it!"

"Not everybody can rise several steps above their class. Father didn't have very much money at the start, and he still doesn't."

"I don't have very much money. I *could* have made a lot of money. I could still make money. But money's not my hang-up. It's not my big thing in life."

"I think it's a combination of not being interested enough in making money, and basically belonging to a certain social class. We're lower middle class, that's who we are. It's like poor people saying, 'Hey, we're poor, that's our lot in life, no shame attached.'"

"Well—I'll buy another lotto ticket tomorrow."

"I was asking you about the kids because there's something about Betty Ann that still seems a mystery to me, and I have a very incomplete memory of it. When Betty Ann was young, I thought of her as the most outgoing, delightful, guaranteed-to-sparkle child. At a certain point, Betty Ann started to become unpopular. I never could understand how the kid who was a world-beater suddenly became the one who gave a party where nobody showed up."

"Oh God, every time I think about that I get sick in the pit of my stomach. I don't know what happened. I blame myself for it. I blame myself for pushing her to take the test that got her into an elite school, Hunter in Manhattan, where it would be impossible for her to make friends. But a lot of that has to do with my upbringing. I had been told for so many years that I was stupid, that I was the schlemiel of the family, that I was a dummy, and the fact that your father had the whole intellectual ball of wax—all he and I wanted from the children was that they should be brilliant and achieve. I used to talk about you children all the time at work. Some guy at Radio Receptor said to me one time: 'All you talk about is what they've accomplished in school. What about their personalities? What about them as people?' And I realized that we were making a big, big mistake. We were pushing intellect, accomplishment, achievement. Daddy used to beat up Lenny in the third grade for not learning his times table fast enough. When that guy at work said that, it frightened me. I was afraid by that time it was already too late.

"Betty Ann started to become very noisy. Her tone became brash and very loud, and she thought that she had to smoke and do provocative things to be popular. She started to have boyfriends. She didn't realize that she was pretty enough and shapely enough and smart enough, that she didn't have to do all that other stuff. I couldn't get through to her about that. And no matter what we said to her, it always hit the wrong note. She had so much—and I don't know what happened. I blame myself."

"I don't think you can blame yourself. Kids have a lot to do with the way they turn out."

"But the other girls in her crowd didn't do that. Then when she went to Hunter for middle school, we lived so far away from Hunter, she made that party and baked all those cupcakes and got everything ready, and nobody came. Oh Phillip, I—when her heart broke, believe me, my heart broke. It was the most horrifying experience that anyone could live through. But their parents didn't let their twelve-year-old girls travel to that part of Brooklyn; they didn't want them to go into Bedford-Stuyvesant. We had got so accustomed to living there, we didn't notice it. But they noticed it."

"What do you remember from that day?"

"The excitement, the cleaning up, the baking, and the waiting. And the waiting. Oh God, the waiting."

"I remember listening for the elevator. The elevator came and closed and the doorbell didn't ring."

"I was sick in the stomach, sick. Oh God, how I felt!"

"Do you think that's why she left Hunter after that?"

"Yes. She was shlepping her schoolbooks in rush hour and she lost an assignment that she worked so hard on. Uhh! She became such a strange person. Not just rebellious. She would do such weird things. She would sneak out of the house in the middle of the night and go wandering in the streets at three, four, or five in the morning. I didn't know it until later. She was only a kid. I didn't know how to comfort her. Because I was too heartbroken myself."

"Do you think she was also being an adventurer, that it came out of a sense of daring, or do you think it was really bitterness? That's what I didn't understand: how come she was bitter so early?"

"Well, why shouldn't she be bitter after a thing like that?"

"You think that the neighborhood was the only reason the girls didn't come—or was it something about her personality that was off-putting?"

"I think it was the neighborhood. That's the reason I gave and I believe it. If I was a parent on the Upper East Side or Upper West Side, I probably wouldn't have let my kids go to Bed-Stuy alone. Those kids weren't like my kids. I was constantly encouraging courage and independence. I tried to live my life. And in trying to live my life, I thrust my children out of the nest. I let you ride the subways early. You had to learn to live your lives. Maybe you were too young. Maybe you might have been ready, but not in the eyes of the rest of the world. My sister once said I was a lazy mother because I sat there and watched Joan climb up on the monkey bars when she was only two or three years old. I thought she should be able to climb up by herself. My sister thought I should get up off my behind and stand there ready to catch her in case she fell. She never did fall. I don't know—I don't really know what I did wrong."

"Why do you keep saying what *you* did wrong? It sounds almost egotistical on your part to take total blame for what happened with Betty Ann."

"She was twelve years old. Who else is there to blame?"

"This is what I've been saying. If you're poor, you can't take it as a personal sin. If you're living in a ghetto, it's not your fault for having no money."

"Tell that to a twelve-year-old girl."

"Well, do you think she blames you?"

"I don't know who she blames. I haven't spoken to her about this for many years," said my mother.

"I asked Betty Ann what she remembered about that whole episode and she dismissed it, saying it was just some snotty kids, it wasn't a big deal. All I can tell you is that I wasn't the person it happened to, and it scarred *me* for life. Just watching it taught me a lesson I will never forget. I made a vow that that would never happen to me. I was terrified! I redoubled my efforts to be ingratiating. I would never trust people enough to give a party and have no one come to it. I would make damn sure I'd know in advance. I would say: 'Hey, you're coming, aren't you?' Somehow I would scope out the situation first. What terrified me was her gullibility: that she could go into it without being aware that no one was going to show up."

"It really must have gone so deep that she prefers not to remember it. Maybe it's just as well for her, not to stomp on her scar issue, because it's not going to help her."

"It's not a question of stomping, it's that all her life she's never been able to deal with feeling unpopular and unloved, and then she acts as though it's not even an issue. She'll wait till she's really down and then she'll say, 'I don't have any friends.' The next time you ask her how she's doing, she acts like there never was a problem."

"Well, that's her philosophy: Don't pay any attention to it and it will go away," said my mother. "She won't seek help; she won't try to find out what's wrong. I can't tell her what's wrong. She gives off a deep sense of falseness. I don't know what the falseness comes from, or what breeding ground is inside her, but it's a phony thing, it's a 'hahaha' laugh that doesn't come from the belly. It's a preoccupation with her looks: like, if she looks gorgeous everyone will drop dead in front of her. It's an arrogance. She doesn't see it. She doesn't understand that the whole world isn't going to fall in love with her."

"And on the other hand, she knows that all too well."

"Unfortunately. I don't know how to deal with it."

"When you said she was going out at three or four in the morning, what else was she doing at that time that was quirky?"

"Oh God, she started taking drugs. She used to go to high school stoned, absolutely stoned, every day."

"How did you handle that?"

"I didn't find out until later. Someone had given me some Miltowns, a tranquilizer, and I couldn't take Miltowns. I took it once; I was like a zombie. And she told me that Miltowns no longer affected her. I didn't know where she was getting it. I'm not the kind of parent who goes looking through her daughter's drawer. I was just hoping that if she was going to go screwing around, she had birth control pills. Although I don't think they had birth control pills at that time. I know that she got a venereal disease. It came out when she took the blood test before she was going to get married to Ezra. Her future mother-in-law found out about it, she had a conniption fit. It was cured at the time. I had told her: 'You can't lie around in a basement in the Village, it's not healthy.' But I couldn't control her, there was nothing I could do about it—"

"You couldn't forbid her to go out? I'm just asking."

"With Betty Ann, if you said up, she'd say down. If I said black, she'd say white. If I said yes, she'd say no. Whatever it was, it had to be the opposite because I was never right. It was partly a symptom of being a teenager. You all had it, to some extent, but sometimes you listened. Sometimes you thought: 'Maybe there's a grain of sense in what Mother is saying.' But with Betty Ann there was never anything I said that could possibly make a difference in her behavior and in her thinking."

"So you mean she didn't respect you."

"Absolutely not. When I walked into the dining room and found her naked with Ezra on the couch, frankly I should have thrown him out. But she had assured me that they were moving in together, so there was nothing I could do about it. I guess I was too lax. Although it would have availed me nothing to throw him out that day anyway. Maybe I shouldn't have thought so much about myself, about my own independence. I should have stayed home and been a strict mother. Do you think that would have worked?"

"Well, I think there's something in-between the two. You *should* have laid down guidelines sometimes a little more, and said: 'No, this isn't right, I don't like this, I don't approve of this.' You wouldn't have had to give up your independence in order to express an opinion like that."

"Oh, I expressed my opinion, but it was like a knife in the water. Or like talking into a wind. All those metaphors."

"Strangely enough, I remember you backing away from a lot of things we did, and I don't think it would have been so terrible for you to have tried to dissuade us from making errors. We were going to make our own errors anyway. But you wouldn't have had to stay home all the time and not work in order to have done that. In some ways it was abnegation on your part: 'What can I say, I've made all kinds of mistakes, who am I to tell you?' I remember a lot of that, instead of: 'No, that's not the way people should behave. Don't do that!'"

"Maybe it's because I had that sort of strict upbringing myself, where everyone said no to me so much that I was stifled and suffocated, until I finally threw it all up and ran away. I couldn't do that to another human being."

"Some parental setting of limits is right to do. Sometimes when a parent says, 'No don't do that,' it's the correct, loving thing."

"Well, I said no when it came to playing with sharp knives. I said no when it came to playing with matches. I said no when it comes to drowning yourself in water."

"What about Father trying to control Betty Ann?"

"He was a nonentity. Although he did call her a tramp. Or a whore."

"I think she remembers that, and is still angry about it."

My sister Betty Ann and I were very close as children. Though she was the younger by a year, she was sharper than me—more advanced, as girls often are at that age than boys—and I was quite dependent on her to show me the ropes, how to tie my shoes and so on. There was also a strong psychic connection, a deep sympathy between us, which lasted well into our twenties. But eventually we had a falling out, after these tapes were made. The shocking fact is that we have not had contact for the last twenty years. Nor does she speak to my brother either. It is as though we boys had monopolized the spotlight the world had to give, leaving her none. I'm sure she would tell you she has her legitimate reasons for having nothing to do with us. Myself, I increasingly experienced her as harsh and shrill, and fooling herself: she would say, for instance, that men shied away from her because she was too strong, too marvelous. She also seemed to want all the bohemian entitlements of an artist without having to take the trouble of making art. Restless, immersing herself in Tibetan Buddhism, changing vocations frequently, from office manager to masseuse to nurse to substitute teacher to insurance claims adjuster, she clearly resented the impertinence of having to make a living, and finally remarried a jewelry maker who would support her; they now live in the country. The alienation of this sibling who had been so loving to me (and I to her) is one of the sorrows and aching mysteries of my life, though I suspect my judgmental attitude toward her missteps—she was fucking up and I called her on it—had a big share of the blame for this estrangement.

"So what was happening to Lenny when he was about fourteen, fifteen?"

"Well, he was in high school. He was having problems with his math and his language. And I couldn't understand why, because here was a bright boy who had taken exams to get into the Honor School, and why was he having problems with two subjects? We went to the school. Daddy mentioned how fantastic he'd been in math and Latin. That's all he had to do; they figured it out in one visit, why Lenny was having these problems. He went to a therapist, Doctor Hendin, I think her name was, someplace on Schermerhorn Street once a week. And he got straightened out." [Interestingly, Lenny remembers it differently: Dr. Hendin told him he should look more to his mother for the source of his problems.] "He took the Regents Scholarship exam and he won a scholarship. He was great at that time. He was so responsible. I don't remember how old he was when Joannie fell down and cut her hand so badly. You looked at the blood and got dizzy, Betty Ann didn't even bother to look, and Lenny wrapped her hand in a towel and took her to the hospital in a taxi. He was cool; he had presence of mind; he knew what he had to do. He had to be responsible, so he was responsible."

"He was raising us kids, to a great extent."

"Yeah. I was working. I went out and got a job so I wouldn't have a nervous breakdown. But I had little kids, so I had to throw a lot of responsibility onto Lenny. Onto you, too. You were also a big boy who watched out for your sisters. On the one hand, I was doing myself a favor, and on the other hand I was filling myself up with guilt. One time I did a show at Lowenstein, we were rehearsing a lot, and Joannie was crying and she had an asthma attack. Lenny said, 'You'd better do what you're doing or she's always going to have an asthma attack as soon as you leave the house.' So I kept doing the show and she got over it, she never had an asthma attack again."

"Pretty smart kid, Lenny. He also had a lot of trouble with Father, right?"

"He did. They fought a lot. I think Daddy went after Lenny not so much to beat him, but because he really wanted to beat me. But he knew that if he ever beat me, I'd kill him."

"Also, in Oedipal terms, Lenny was supplanting him. He was the man of the family in a lot of ways; he was raising the kids. So he *was* Father's rival. Look, I never felt when I was growing up that I had to do battle with Father. I always felt that if there was a battle to be fought, it was with Lenny. Lenny was the father figure. He was the one who laid down the law; he took care of me; he explained things."

"If you're not going to be there as a father, someone had to. But Father couldn't accept that. In spite of the fact he wasn't there, he still didn't want to accept it."

"And then Lenny had a temper also. It wasn't all one way. I used to wonder, why did Lenny allow himself to be baited by Father into getting in a fistfight? Father could have said anything to me; I wasn't going to slug it out with him."

"I think Lenny wanted to get physical. He wanted to fight. He was also asserting his territorial rights. It was like two bucks locking their horns. I would try to get between them and pull them apart. Because no matter that Lenny was younger, Daddy was much stronger. I mean, he could have hurt Lenny. He could knock his head and do something very bad. I didn't want that. Listen, he's my son."

"I'm glad you did. I would be horrified if, looking back to that time, I didn't think that you had tried to stop it."

"Ridiculous, that kind of violence. I mean every once in a while I'd give you a slap in the head, but I didn't use it all the time. I used it more as a threat."

"You told me you thought that Father could black out at times and lose control."

"I think so. And the only way he could show his dominance was over someone who was weaker."

"What was Joannie like as a little kid?"

"Joannie was very active, the kind of baby that had to be tied to her crib. Even then, she managed to get out; I don't know how. We had a curtain between the bedroom and the living room. I would look up and I would see these pale little yellow toes at the bottom of the curtain. She would get out of bed and stand holding onto the bed and she'd rock, and listen to the radio, when she was seven or eight months old. Joannie was a skinny cuddle-bunny. She was small for her age and wore Betty Ann's castoffs. She was thin and pale and green and she looked sickly. Betty Ann sparkled, with those spit curls and blue eyes, and she would skip, skip, skip—never stay put. Betty Ann was a tap dancer, Joannie was a ballet dancer. Joannie was very anemic. She was not an eater. No matter what I did, the food didn't sit well on her. She couldn't gain weight."

"I was also skinny, and had to be put on a milk shake and spaghetti diet to fatten me up. Remember?"

"Yeah, but when you were two years old and I had pictures taken, you sat down and your little penis went all the way in, because there was so much fat around it, that the man said, 'Look he's got two navels.'" [laughs]

## *The Gay Crowd*

When my mother began performing, first in the Lowenstein company shows and later in musical revues put on in church basements and hotels, she brought Bob Waxman and his boyfriends home to our cluttered apartment on the cusp of Fort Greene and Bedford Stuyvesant. At thirteen, in this, my first exposure to theater folk and uncloseted homosexuals, I was both fascinated and on guard. My mother, though, was clearly in her element, appreciating these gay men and appreciated in turn by them.

"Let's get back to you and Bob Waxman. You did a few shows with him?"

"We had a helluva good time, and we socialized. It bothered Bob that every time he wanted me to come over, Daddy was always there. There was always a barrier between us. I guess in the end I really didn't want to be such a part of that gay crowd. Had I had a different kind of husband, someone who was more—more fun, it wouldn't have been so bad. We could have had a lot of fun together, because there was always a party or a movie to go to, always something doing. But to spend time with me and have to spend it with *him,* Bob didn't want it. Because Daddy would sit there and fall asleep. All of a sudden people would stop what they were saying and turn around and see this man on a sofa fast asleep. That's not cool. I was stuck with that, and Bob didn't think it was funny. He stopped inviting me because he didn't want to have to invite Daddy."

"Why didn't you go alone?"

"Well, many times I did. But I didn't always want to have to go home alone, and there was not always a place to park up there, and there were times when I was between cars and I didn't want to have to spend money for taxis. Also, I didn't want to get that far into the gay crowd. If I went alone all the time, I'd be accepted with the rest of his friends, who were all gay."

"So you didn't want to be, to use that crude expression, a 'fag hag'?"

"I didn't want to be a fag hag. I'd spent enough time there, and I looked with distaste at the straight ones who did hang around them all the time."

"And yet you fit very well into that gay world."

"Oh sure, when we were working, then we'd have a lot of fun. But when it dragged on too long . . . Maybe I don't have that much tolerance. Or maybe I just get bored with people after a while. I think that's what happened. I got tired of them."

"Was it an adjustment for you? I doubt you had been around that many homosexuals growing up."

"No, in fact I didn't know any. But no, there were no adjustments. It didn't mean anything to me. I knew that they were different, and I knew why they were different. But I didn't know the real extent of their private lives. I always knew the guys went after guys and the girls went after girls. And I thought in some cases it was a damn shame because some of the girls were so beautiful, and some of the guys were so handsome. But—that's what they wanted. They never had any kind of influence on me and my life. Bob tried to have an influence on you kids. He wanted very much to get hold of you. He figured Lenny was a lost cause. But you he wanted. And I didn't think he stood a chance. He tried to be as charming as he could to you, and you, being a polite teenager, smiled and were polite. But you didn't—dig it. It was as simple as that. He gave up."

I must say, this comes as a stunning surprise. I remember Bob voiced a certain tender interest in me, but I interpreted it at the time as avuncular rather than predatory. There was one night when my mother and Bob and I had gone up on the roof of our apartment building to catch a summer breeze, and I had confessed that I still hadn't gotten any pubic hair. Puberty was coming late for me, at fourteen, and it had me concerned. He told me not to worry: "You will, it will come." He was very reassuring that I would be a man, fully a man. I remember one time he noticed I had dandruff. I was always frightened of his way of zeroing in on physical appearance. I said to him: 'Well, what can you do about it?' He said, 'Maybe you're shampooing your hair too much.' I had to smile, because, quite the contrary, I was barely conscious of shampoo at that time. I was just taking showers and washing my hair with soap. In that way, I learned from Bob elliptically, broaching subjects with him that I couldn't have with my own father, even as I continued to feel threatened by the encroaching gay milieu. In years to come, when I had gay friends, I would be thankful for this early exposure.

"Do you think he felt rejected by me?" I asked my mother.

"No, I think all gay guys are gonna try. They're gonna look at every attractive kid and give it a whirl. If it works, okay. If it doesn't, so it doesn't."

"Did you feel any sort of responsibility towards Lenny and me, as far as whether you were doing the right thing, having this guy hang around your two sons?"

"Not at all. Absolutely none. I never felt that I was exposing you to an unnatural life. I had all the confidence in the world that you would not go gay."

"I don't know that it's an issue of confidence, because that implies that if I had gone gay it would have been wrong. Neither of us was disposed to go gay but—"

"Let's just say I had all the confidence in the world that you were not disposed to go gay. All right? I'll put it that way."

"First he was interested in Lenny?"

"No, I think too many girls were chasing Lenny. When he first met Lenny, Lenny was already going to Pratt, and the girls in Lowenstein who had been working on the show were making eyes at him and he was making eyes back. But you were younger, three years younger than Lenny. He was seventeen, and you were fourteen, and that was just the age for Bob to go tippy-toe creeping up and stalking someone. But you just smiled politely in your way; it was thanks but no thanks. I don't even know if you were aware that he was stalking you."

"I wasn't. Nor was I aware that you felt distant from Bob. I thought you definitely got along better with those guys, that they were a kind of second family to you. I thought that you took to it like a duck to water."

"Of course the one thing you didn't realize was that I did it pretty much to keep other men away. Having had the experience of Benno and Willy, and my brother-in-law Morris, and sundry other gentlemen, I felt that surrounding myself with gay men like that was protection. To me it was like getting fat. When I got older, and I didn't even want gay men around me, I surrounded myself with physical fat as protection. But of course you couldn't possibly have known that."

"But why would you do that? Were they so terrible, your relations with men that you had to—"

"I didn't want any more relationships with men. I didn't want the problems that having an affair would bring. It was too much trouble, and my whole feeling was, I can't be bothered. I could have had some real terrific times when I was on the road later, in show business. But I couldn't be bothered with the problems that another man would bring. What I had at home wasn't terrific or groovy, but I reconciled myself to that, prepared myself for celibacy, which was just about what I had, and that was it. I locked myself away in an emotional convent by surrounding myself with people who were no threat to me."

"That seems like a real personality change, very different from when you were still looking for some kind of love outside the marriage."

"The only one I had after that was Herbie, but that wasn't love."

"But something must have happened to make you change so."

"I realized that there was nothing I could do about my situation. I was hog-tied, finished, and as far as that was concerned, my life was over."

"After I got married the first time, I always felt Bob was a little angry at me. Of course, now I see the most obvious explanation was that I got married!" I said.

"Sure. He had that problem with little Bobby too. You remember Little Bobby?"

"No."

"Little Bobby was no great bargain. The only thing little Bobby had was an enormous thing between his legs. Strangely enough, Waxman pushed little Bobby and Martha together, and he and Bobby separated, and little Bobby turned out to be a terrific husband."

"Bob Waxman was also going out with a guy named Abe at that time, wasn't he?" I suddenly remembered Abe, this redheaded, soft-spoken young man with long red eyelashes and numerous freckles.

"Bob was with Abe when we were doing the first show. Bob came over one time when we were living on Washington Avenue, and we went to one of those little triangle vest-pocket parks, and he sat down in sort of a drizzly way, he was crying bitter tears because Abe could not return his love. He hated Abe's mother because Abe's mother wanted him to go straight and settle down. She pushed him into therapy. Abe's mother hated Bob, and Bob hated her. Then Abie got married. But—it didn't take. He left, and went back to being gay."

"I always felt that you were amused by gay men. That somehow their lusts and needs had something comic about them to you."

"I was amused at the beginning, but then I found out that their needs and their loves were not amusing. They're just as painful and just as serious as heterosexuals' loves and lusts and needs. I . . . I feel sorry for them, many of them. Then you get a couple like Jay and David [Jay was my mother's sometime theater director] who have been together almost thirty years, which is longer than most heterosexual couples I know in show business anyway. Just the fact that Jay used to get the young busboys in his room at the hotel and have a little *mufky-fufky*, as they say. . . . I said, 'How could you do that, you love your man and he's probably faithful to you,' and he said: 'Sex has nothing to do with love. This is not being unfaithful. If you get horny, you get laid. What the hell difference does it make? It doesn't mean I'm going to love David any less.' I said to myself: 'Goddamn it, why didn't I think like that twenty-five years ago? Why did I let my life be ruled by that Victorian morality I was stuck with? If I'd thought like that, my life would have been a whole lot different. Oh boy!'"

"What eventually happened between you and Bob Waxman?"

"I broke away from Bob. There was a time I didn't see him for a long time."

"Why?"

"Let me back up a bit. Lowenstein had fired Bob and replaced him with a woman by the name of Lila Garrett, who had no imagination, absolutely none. She was hired to get the show together for Lowenstein."

"Why was Bob fired?"

"Someone had written a poison pen letter and signed his name to it. The company thought he had done it. We said: 'No way. Bob Waxman does not write poison pen letters. If he wants to say something nasty to you, he will say it to your face.' They wanted him out anyway because they thought he was a troublemaker. So meanwhile, we got together with this company in Brooklyn that had only done stage plays; they wanted to do a musical revue. He gave me a song to sing, and I was delighted. One day I get a notice from Lowenstein to go to this honcho's office. So I went. He asked me to be in the show directed by Lila Garrett. I said: 'First of all, they want me to be in the chorus. I don't want to be in the chorus. I'm used to being a star.' Then he came out with this fantastic remark, which I will never forget: 'Management will look with disfavor on anyone who does a show with Bob Waxman.' Well, knowing me, that's the worst thing he could have said, because I don't scare. Of course the other amateur sopranos got scared, and they withdrew from Bob's show. But I didn't. I said to this executive: 'From nine to five, I belong to Lowenstein; that's what you pay me for. I give every bit of effort to my job. After five, I belong to me, and you don't dare tell me what to do with my time.' He said, 'They won't like that.' I said, 'That's too bad.' Today, I would say 'Fuck you.' At that time, I didn't use that kind of language. I said, 'They're going to have to live with it,' and I walked away. I did the show with Bob.

"To be able to sing and act in an amateur capacity was wonderful, everything was terrific. He then had the opportunity to take a part of the show and make a small revue out of it, and do it on a commercial basis. And he told me quite frankly he couldn't use me. I was too old. And it hurt. I felt he had betrayed me. Even though he wanted to keep up our friendship, I didn't want it. Because I felt he had hurt me, I stopped seeing him. He also did the show *Pins and Needles,* which I certainly could have been in. He never called me. I said, 'Okay, if that's the way he wants it, that's the way he'll have it.' And I didn't see him anymore. Then *he* called. He started up again. No, wait, I called him, because I wanted to take singing lessons again."

"Didn't you do a nightclub act with him at some point?"

"Yes. Bob wanted me to do it, and I did. He got a few numbers together. I sang and he accompanied me on piano. I was so terribly nervous. I was terrified. However, there was someone in the audience, Gus Schirmer, who was related to the Schirmer sheet music family, and who said he was going to do everything for me. He told me I was absolutely divine. I was the best thing since—halvah. Whatever. He was going to find a singing teacher for me. Gus Schirmer sent me to a woman teacher in Brooklyn, and I started working with her, and she started bringing the voice up, making it very classical. Classical to the point, and big to the point, that when I sang, the glasses in her mother's china closet started tinkling and shaking and we had to stop. I said, 'Are you sure you didn't rig that?' So I had the voice now when I wanted it. However, Gus didn't have anything for me, with a voice like that. That I couldn't understand. He was very impressed when I was doing the pop stuff that Bob had given me to sing, but when I was doing the other stuff . . . I mean let's face it, I'm no Shirley Jones. That's the one he had discovered. That was his big star.

"So I auditioned around, and I got a small role in a show on Long Island. Just before I signed the contract, Equity pulled the plug. They called a strike, and when the strike was over the producers sent me a very nice letter, telling me they were sorry but they can't use me. They're not going to give out any temporary cards. I didn't want a temporary card; I wanted to join the union! The result was that I didn't get in when I had the chance to. And I blame

Gus Schirmer for that. He had the chance to do it for me, and he didn't do it. Anyway, I was heartbroken. I didn't do anything for a long time. That's when I stopped seeing Bob. I was working at Best Coats and Aprons for three years. I left there and went over to Lynnsbrook Fabrics. In Lynnsbrook, that's when I called him again. I went over to his house, and we spent a nice hour. He said, 'You've got a classical voice; it's getting bigger and stronger. It's good for musical comedy, but that's about it.' What can you do with a voice like that? He found music that would be good for roles I could play, that were suitable for me. He studied *The Boy Friend,* Madame Dubonnet's music, and other parts. Then he suggested, because I still suffered from stage fright, that I take some courses in acting. He felt that the HB Studio on Bank Street would be a good place for me to go. I did, I went over there and I did some sort of sense-memory stuff for half a semester, which was really just fun, and then a semester of scene study. The kids, they loved me: if they needed someone to play a mother, I was the mother. The last day of the semester, which was on a Wednesday, the teacher pulled me aside, he said I was a natural actor, I really should take advantage of the talent that I had—and do it!

"The next day, Thursday, I bought *Backstage.* They had an ad for a replacement for Madame Dubonnet in *The Boy Friend.* I had studied the music, and they said they wanted a heavyset woman! [laughs] I fit the description. I called and set up an appointment for the following day, which was a Friday. That Thursday I went out and I bought makeup that I had never worn before. I bought false eyelashes and eyeliners and eye shadow and rouge and lipstick and nail polish. I tell you, I really was something.

"The next day, Friday, I got myself all *fatootsed.* Now, without my glasses I'm blind. So I met Albert, who became my seeing eye dog, and we walked up to the Ed Sullivan Building. He took me by the hand and walked with me up Broadway to the office, we came upstairs and there I met this marvelous director, Jay. The pianist was there, and I sang a little something for him. He asked me if I knew the songs for that part, and I said yes. But unfortunately I had left my glasses in my purse, and my purse was out in the outer office with Al, and I was in the inner office and I couldn't see, and I didn't remember the words to the intro. I had practiced the song without the intro. So there I was, looking down at the piano, squinting on one knee, until I reached the part where the intro was over. Then I was able to stand up and really sing. He sat there in front of me with this expression on his face, like he was pulling the music out of me. The more he did that, the more I gave. My voice got prettier and bigger and clearer. I stopped being nervous. As long as he was there, I felt so confident; all my nervousness went away. I just sang to him, and he loved it. He said, 'Okay, just sing the other songs.' I sang all the others, and he said, 'Okay you've got a job.' When they picked me up off the floor, I was ready to sign the contract.

"I walked out of an office job that was paying considerably more than any job I'd ever had. Close to two hundred dollars a week, and that was sixteen years ago—1968, I think. I was fifty years old. And I went to work for eighty dollars a week. Singing dancing *ecting*! [in a Yiddish accent] That's what I wanted to do. I didn't care if they'd offered me fifty dollars a week; I would have gone. I was walking on a cloud. It was the Friday before Labor Day, so I couldn't go back to the office and give notice because everyone had gone home already. I didn't know what to do with myself. I called Bob. I called my acting teacher. Tuesday after Labor Day, I went to the office and gave my two weeks' notice. All the salesmen figured I was going to another textile company. I had a friend there, Alex, who was also interested in getting into show business, and when I told him, one of the salesmen heard me. He said, 'You're going to do *what*?' When the word got around that I was going to go on the road to act, all of a sudden everyone was collected around my desk. Everyone was talking to me as if I was a different person! Can you explain that?"

"The desperation in their own lives? The dreams they didn't realize? I don't know. One of them made it."

"Of course Alex didn't. Alex got stuck; he got married. Had a couple of kids, got divorced, and now he's going with some other girl. He always wanted to . . . He still calls me, still comes to see me. Still takes acting lessons. And he's still so handsome. [sighs] It's a very strange—I felt embarrassed by all their attention. And that's why, when I met a theater owner who used to say 'Actors are a dime a dozen, you could treat them like shit and get away with it,' I wasn't used to that kind of treatment. I think one of the worst was the fat guy in Houston who owned that theater. All he had to do was give us one meal a week. We had different contracts after that, where we used to get fed every day. But he fed us only one day a week, on Sunday. He used to stand there and make sure that we didn't get seconds, and that a slice of roast beef wasn't too big. If it was too thick, we would hear about it. He was so gross—*that* was a fat man!"

"Did you have any problem with vocal production? As I remember, you had a sweet little voice, and it was hard for you to get the volume."

"When I worked on my voice, really worked on it, I had the volume. But I never worked at it enough. It's really hard; it's tough. I didn't know how to control my lungs, or do anything with breath. And Bob was not a good enough teacher, so I always got laryngitis. That means I was not pressing my voice right."

"Did you feel at that time that if you really worked hard you could make yourself a first-rate singer?"

"I don't know what you call a 'first-rate singer.' That's subjective."

"I mean, a professional."

"The minute I walked into Jay's office and signed a contract I became a professional."

"So you went very far on a good ear and a natural melodic sense, without actually the technique, just on native ability."

"Yeah, I did have native ability. And I had just enough training and just enough ambition. But I didn't have enough push to keep going at it. There are women my age who can really sing up a storm. I hear them and I see them, but—I'm tired. I remember this great contralto, she was doing a concert at seventy. She wore high-laced shoes up to her knees. And a gorgeous evening gown, right down to the floor. She was sitting backstage with her hair all done up like a Grecian goddess; she was gray by that time, with all these diamonds and rhinestones, and her dress up to her thighs. When she got up to sing, God it could break your heart, it was so beautiful."

"Whatever happened to Bob Waxman?"

"Bob's family was fabulously wealthy. Bob is a millionaire now, a multimillionaire because he sold those little motels and theaters that they had in Atlantic City when his father and his Uncle Henry died; he was able to sell off all this property to the big casinos. So he and Rock, I understand, have a very nice house out in Long Island."

## *Grandpa Leaves Some Money*

"Grandpa, the old fucker, finally died. He left some money to his children, Arthur and Al. Arthur didn't need it, but he took it. Your Uncle Bernie [a retired cop, the son of Grandpa's first wife] wasn't his child, but Bernie had done an awful lot for him, more than he deserved. He fed him; he clothed him. Grandpa didn't leave anything to him. But between Daddy and Arthur, they decided to give something to Bernie anyway, a couple of hundred dollars. There was just enough left over to buy a co-op on 636 Brooklyn Avenue, in Flatbush. I think it was something like a twenty-five hundred dollar down payment. We picked the apartment we liked and we moved in. It was quite a move up. And then we lost it. I don't know why we finally moved out. I think the maintenance went so high we couldn't afford it."

"What was Father's reaction when his father died?"

"I don't know—he never showed his feelings He was always very proud of the fact that he never cried. When Lenny went away to high school, Daddy took my finger to feel the tear that was running down his face. I thought that was so disgusting—I don't know why, it turned my stomach. 'Don't tell me how emotional you are! Or don't tell me how emotional you're *not,* and then prove to me you are. I'm not interested.' By the time Lenny graduated high school, I had no respect, no love, no even *liking,* no interest in the man at all. But this business of 'I never cry, here, feel my tears'—it was awful, awfully embarrassing. Anyway, I don't know what he felt when his father died."

"I remember we were actually celebrating right after Grandfather died."

"Whoopee! You're darned right. And you didn't go to the funeral either. I didn't want you to. I didn't even want to have to go. But I did. So we moved into Brooklyn Avenue. And Glen Fuller from Lowenstein sold me his Dodge Dart for a hundred dollars. I didn't know how to drive. I took driving lessons. I went to get my driver's license. As luck would have it, the doctor said: 'You have got to get to the hospital. If you don't get to the hospital this week, you are not going to live till next week.' I had to have a hysterectomy, I was bleeding to death. I had been having hemorrhages every three weeks instead of regular periods every four weeks. That was when my sister Gladys said I had the operation so I wouldn't have to go to her son Lawrence's wedding. Anyway, I couldn't drive for a couple of months. It was an old car with a stick shift. I learned how to drive on it. I had fun. I enjoy driving so much."

"I thought you were going to tell about how you bribed the driving instructor."

"Yeah, I can't take a test. The first test I took, I was fine, actually, but it was the inspector's first day on a new job, and HE was scared. He was so nervous that even though he didn't have to, he kept hitting the brakes. So by the time we got ready to do the back-park, he was driving me crazy. I failed the test. The second one, I was so nervous with this moron in the car with me, that I did absolutely everything badly. The third one just happened to be in the middle of a snowstorm. And it was the same inspector. The snow was piled so high that there wasn't a question of seeing the curb—you couldn't see no matter whether you were going left or right. He said, 'Don't bother with the back-park. You can't see the sidewalk; I can't see the sidewalk either. Forget it.' I'd been told all I had to do was leave an envelope on the seat. And I didn't even have to have left that forty dollars for him, because no matter who was there, I would have done it perfectly. The fact that I paid him was simply because I was told it would be a good idea. But what the hell, he got his forty bucks, I got my license, and everything was fine. I still don't think I back-park too good."

"Getting back to Brooklyn Avenue, what was life like there for you?"

"I worked. I had a lover who used to come and see me, Herbert. You guys went to school. You graduated. Then we lost the co-op. We started living on that place on Nostrand Avenue, a real hole in the wall, where you and Lenny slept down in the basement. And Daddy had a stroke. I had plans to go to California. I had been offered a transfer to California, and that's probably why we sold the co-op on Brooklyn Avenue. Frankly I should have gone. But my family made my decision for me. I couldn't go because Betty Ann was still in high school."

"When Father had his stroke, what was that like?"

"Well, we had just moved to Nostrand Avenue, we had just bought the old secondhand Ford, and I decided to take a trip with Betty Ann and Joan. So the three of us got in the car and we went to New England. We visited my brother George, my sister-in-law Ida; we rode all around and had a wonderful time. I decided it's time I moved out. 'I'm going to get an apartment of my own. You want to come with me, girls? It's not going to be a big apartment. We'll speak to the boys. If they want to come with me, fine. If they don't want to come with me, *azai gezunt*.' But either way, I felt I had to leave him after sticking it out for so many years. It was time. They agreed. Everyone thought it was wonderful. You kids always agreed with me. 'We're very supportive, Mother. Anything you do, we're behind you, pushing you.' But when it comes to doing anything, forget it! However . . ."

"What were we supposed to do?"

"Well, at that time there was nothing you could do. Now, there's something more you can do—but I'll get to that some other time. However. We got home, and we waited a couple of days. Daddy as usual went to bed early. And you kids and I had a small conference about my leaving. I had a feeling he heard us, although we kept it very low. First he called, 'Turn down the TV.' I don't know if you remember that, in a very high voice. We had the TV on so he couldn't hear what we were saying. Four o'clock in the morning, he got up to go to the bathroom and fell right on his ass. I picked him up and I walked with him to the bathroom. I held him in front of the toilet, and he peed, I took him back, got him into bed, and he was shivering. I piled all the blankets on top of him. I didn't know what was wrong with him. In the morning, he was very strange. I called the doctor, and he didn't know what was wrong. I called his brother, called his brother's doctor: *he* didn't know what was wrong. So I called an ambulance, and took him to the hospital. And that was it. Betty Ann stood there against the wall, crying, 'Mama, we can't leave him now. How can we leave him now?' And I said, 'Oh my God, here I go again.'"

"I have a strange memory. He was suspicious when he had a stroke that you were trying to kill him." [I do remember his fear and mistrust of my mother that time. We had all been reading Tanizaki's novel, *The Key,* in which a married couple tried to polish each other off, and that, plus his extreme frailty, may have contributed to his suspicious reaction.]

"Yes, he got scared, and everyone was getting hysterical, and finally I had to call an ambulance to take him to the hospital. My doctor who never made house calls did come, and said it was Bell's Palsy. Couldn't be Bell's Palsy; I'd seen people with Bell's Palsy, with one eye hanging down. His face was not hanging down; it's just that he couldn't move one side. They took him to the hospital. He was there for about two months. The hospital was close enough we could walk over and see him. Even when we came, he would complain that we didn't sneak up before visiting hours. What would be the purpose in coming to see him two-and-a-half hours a day instead of two hours a day? And you know what a drag he is, what a pain he is. You people didn't want to go. Nobody wanted to go see him. So you went and stayed a couple of minutes and left.

"Your father's stroke had been caused by a cigarette cough. He coughed so hard one time that it closed up the artery in his neck—the carotid artery, I think they call it—and it stopped the blood flow momentarily, and *that* caused the stroke. He had always, always smoked very heavily. I had stopped. Not stopped completely, but

I was always a light smoker. He would buy seven cartons, I would buy three, and that would last a week. So in the hospital he was told not to smoke, not to eat butter, and to keep away from high-cholesterol foods. He was also given a rubber ball to squeeze, because he was very weak. He was told to do isometric exercises at the wall, to walk up the wall with his fingers, to buy a pulley with ropes for his arms. We got everything that he was supposed to use and installed them and he never used them. He was in the hospital and his birthday was coming up. He was upset; he was crying. He was moaning and groaning that he wanted to go home. Finally, one day, the doctor said to him, 'Can you walk?' He said yes, though he hadn't been. The doctor said, 'If you can walk, you can go home.' He got out of the wheelchair, and he walked two or three steps and landed on his ass. But because he was so determined with his birthday coming up, they sent him home, which was a big mistake, because he should have stayed for therapy. They told me to bring him in for therapy. I tried to bring him in; he didn't want to go. He only wanted to go back to work, and he wasn't ready to go back to work."

"But he did get his walking back, right?"

"Yeah. He walked. He finally walked."

"So he must have exercised in some way . . ."

"Only walking. But he needed his arms, he needed his upper body, and he refused to exercise *that*. His head was fine, and they took him back to work, because with half a brain he was still smarter than the guys they had hired to take his place when he was out. That I will always give him. Smart he was. That was the one thing that intrigued me about him in the first place. He was not handsome; he was not rich. He was smart, and I was always fascinated by intelligent people. I always thought I could learn from them. It would be like getting educated without having to go to school. And he had so much to teach. So he went back to work."

"What was it like for you during this period, the night he had the stroke and after, the following weeks?"

"The night that he had the stroke was awful. I was up with him all night. We had twin beds at the time, and I was moving him from one bed to the other, because he was wetting himself. I would put out plastic sheets on each bed . . . I couldn't get him to the bathroom; I couldn't lift him after that first time he fell on the floor. There was no way that I could handle it, so I kept moving him from one bed to the other. It was all night long. You kids came up from downstairs to help, but I don't think you stayed. You went back to sleep. I know the girls didn't go back to sleep. For me it was agony. I didn't know what to do; there was no way I could help him. And all I felt at the time was, 'Oh my God, another burden, just when I wanted out. Now I'm stuck.' I resented the hell out of that burden. Every time he got sick again, I resented it more. I couldn't feel sorry for him, because it was someone I—I didn't like, I didn't care for. This burden was foisted off on me. That's what made it harder: I had to take care of him, had to clean him up. I had no nurses, I had no visiting people, I had nobody to help me."

"Well, let's say a year after he went back to work, what would have prevented you from leaving him then?"

"When we moved out of there, into the big apartment on Nostrand Avenue, then I went into show business, and I was able to get away from him. Months at a time. So it didn't matter. It was fun. I was doing something that I enjoyed. I wasn't making any money."

"It sounds like he was supporting you."

"He was supporting himself. I was away on the road; I was supporting myself. I was traveling, all my expenses were being taken care of, I was no expense to him, I was able to put something aside. And I always sent money home. So he wasn't supporting me! What I do appreciate is the fact that after working all those years and putting money aside, I was able to use the savings account to take my pictures and print my resumes and things like that. And he *was* supportive of my acting career. But he had no choice, you see. I had finally decided that it was my turn. When Lenny wanted art school, he went to art school; when you wanted to go to Columbia, you did. Everyone got what they wanted, while I waited it out. When it was my turn to go, I felt: okay. It *had* to be, because I was so desperate it was either that or suicide."

## *On the Road*

"Can you tell me about that early period when you first went on the road?"

"Oh that first show, *The Boy Friend*? We flew for the first time in my life on one of these little airlines; I think it was Piedmont. It's the kind where you have to stick your foot out the window to get it to stop, and it's put together with elastic bands. We flew to Jackson, Mississippi, to join the cast there. The woman who I was replacing was heavyset, a very pretty young woman, and she was having a thing with the romantic lead that I was supposed to act with. I was trying to rehearse, and every time they would go off together to New Orleans or somewhere, and I'm trying to learn my lines and learn the dances. Anyway, it took me about ten days, and I managed to get down as much as possible. Then everyone piled into cars and drove to Houston. I opened in *The Boy Friend* in Houston. The first performance, I did the whole thing like I was in a coma. I still have that review. Not a good one. It picked up after that; it was fine. It lasted five weeks. I broke my toe because someone dropped a chair on me. I had laryngitis too. I never really knew how to pace my voice. So we were supposed to go on to Albuquerque, but we didn't. Jay got disgusted, canceled, broke us up, and brought us home. Jay had had very little contact with me at that time. We got along fine, but some of the other cast members were terrible singers or doing terrible things. There was one guy who was supposed to catch the girl but he just walked away. When she started going back, she must have seen him leave out of the corner of her eye, because otherwise she would have fallen and broken her spine. Or cracked her head."

"Jay doesn't sound like he was able to control them very well."

"He was in New York rehearsing another show. When he started the new company and made me stage manager, they toed the line. I would go in there and say, 'Either you clean up or you'll have no water. I'll turn off the water.' Oh, I was tough. I had to be. Actors are often irresponsible. They're stupid, and if you're not tough with them, they walk all over you. That's why he liked me as a stage manager. Anyway, I fell in love with the stage. I can't tell you the feeling—or maybe you can know the feeling, like when you saw your first story in *The Paris Review,* or listed among *The Best Stories of 1975*? That rush, that thrill, that feeling in your stomach—it's indescribable. I learned that I could handle it, that I could tour, that I was good at it; I enjoyed it. And I was determined to keep going with it."

"How did you act with the broken toe? Did you have to sit?"

"It was awful. That night I broke it, I was really in pain. I got a hairline fracture. They taped it to the big toe, so I was able to walk—painfully. But in that show, I had to do two roles. I had to play both Madame Dubonnet and Lady Brackhurst. I had to shift from a French accent to a British accent. When I became Lady Brackhurst, I had to change my whole persona. I put on a big straw hat so that you couldn't see the black wig I was wearing as Madame Dubonnet, and put on a simple frumpy old coat down to the floor. I put on black, heeled shoes, but I borrowed a cane. They cut out the scenes that Madame Dubonnet and Lady Brackhurst had together. That would have been a trick, but Jay was very inventive. To have to walk with my toe bandaged up and with my laryngitis—I think I found just about every emergency room along the tour.

"I came home, and I said to myself: 'This is it. I'm never going back to an office. I'm not going to pound a typewriter anymore in my whole life. I'm not going to have bosses making demands. Any time I'm going to have demands made on me, it will be by my director, and it's going to be what *I* want to do.' So I called some of the people that I had known in acting school. One of them mentioned that he had a TV connection. He told me the kind of letters to write, and who to see in the agencies. He was very helpful. He put me on videotape. I really hate to see myself on videotape. He told me how to do some print work. He got me started. The first commercial I made was a print ad for Benson & Hedges, where I was dressed as a Valkyrie. Then there was the Alka-Seltzer commercial. After that, I was just going like a house on fire. I made two or three commercials in the space of two weeks; I did print work. I was going from one thing to another. I had all this marvelous makeup—they let me keep the eyelashes on—and a hair piece. I was Queen of the May. I made a lot of money, and I had a lot of fun. I met a lot of wonderful people. And then somehow it all dried up. They started wanting spokespeople who were not as ethnic. It went from one extreme to the other. The ethnic people had to speak ethnically; I can't speak ethnically. If they were doing an Italian mama commercial, they had to have the Italian accent, which I don't have. Even if I had the Italian looks, I didn't have the Italian feel."

"What about the Jewish feel?"

"They weren't looking for Jews, because Jews weren't 'in.' Italian was 'in.' Italian is still 'in.' I don't like Italians. Maybe it's my Bostonian background, or maybe it's my German roots, or maybe it's just my own personality, that cannot tolerate that effusive . . . It's one thing to see it depicted by Anna Magnani. But if I were to see someone that's not in a movie carrying on like that in the street, I would be embarrassed. I know very few Italians that I can tolerate. One happens to be an actress who lives in my building, a lovely woman. But she doesn't have that peasant Italian quality; she has a high lovely beautiful speaking voice."

"So you're just against peasant Italians."

"I find it embarrassing, all that excitement and—"

"Earthiness."

"Is that what it is, earthiness?"

"Yeah. Anna Magnani is very earthy."

"I don't like it in Jewish people either. I can't stand all that with the hands and the loud voices and the hollering and carrying on and the pulling of hair and the biting of fingers. Maybe I was meant to live among the Irish, who are very contained. Or the English. I just find that other style very offensive."

This just goes to show how little she knew about the Irish. In the face of her prejudiced statements about ethnic groups, I had nothing to say. Why fight it? "So what was it like being a pretend Italian?"

"If you remember, in the Alka-Seltzer ad or the Levy's Jewish Rye ad, I didn't have to do anything; all I had to do was smile. Every other time they sent me to audition as an Italian, it had to be the other, more vocal kind. I couldn't deal with it and I couldn't do it. So I refused to go for the audition. It was as simple as that. When they called me for auditions, I would say, 'If it's for an Italian mama, thank you but I don't think I want it.' I had my nose fixed. I just won't go anymore. 'Don't call me.' And they stopped calling me."

"It sounds like you've walked away from a lucrative career."

"Not at all. I would see who my competition was; whenever I used to go I knew that I could never compete with real Italians. When they opened their mouths, I knew they were the ones who were going to be chosen. They had the real foreign accent, and they belonged to the Italian union. So okay, I'll be an extra. I'll make my hundred dollars a day. Leave me alone. I'm not hung up on money, thank God, because if I were hung up on money, I would go and kill for commercials. I would have lost fifty pounds; I would have tinted my hair again. I would have had a face-lift. I would have done a lot of things if I was that hung up on money. I'm not. I'm sixty-six years old now. I want to grow old gracefully. Leave me in peace."

"We're not talking about now, but ten years ago—"

"Ten years ago I was doing fine. I was working on the stage. I prefer the stage. It's much more interesting than to work on a commercial. Commercials only mean money. Someone comes running in and says, 'Mom, tennis is my life! How can you wash my clothes in that ordinary detergent?' Like it's a big surprise. Woopy-doo. I can't say those things; they stick in my craw. I'd laugh. They're stupid! But there are people who can say them and sound serious. I have integrity [laughs]. Maybe that's it."

"Didn't you come up for a job with *The Godfather* at one point?"

"With *The Godfather* I was only a stand-in for Morgana King. I was an extra, a face in the crowd. The time I was up for a part and they decided they needed a real Italian, it was *Lovers and Other Strangers*. The funny thing is, they wanted me to play the role of Bea Arthur's sister. She's as Italian as I am. It was all right for *her* to do it, because she sounds Italian even though she's not. They couldn't use me, because although I looked Italian I didn't sound Italian, and they had to have a woman who could speak a few Italian words. So that's why I lost out."

"I still can't believe that there were never any Jewish mother parts. I don't think there's been a blackout of Jewish parts in the last fifteen years or so. May not be as many parts as Italians, but—"

"Well, in the last few years I simply withdrew altogether. I stopped my answering service too. The thing is, I like the stage better. To me the stage is more gratifying, because it's instant satisfaction. If you know that you've gotten your part down right, and you know you're good—and I know I'm good onstage—then you'll never get a bad review. Except for that first time in Houston, when I looked like I was in a coma—that was the only time I ever got a bad review. Jay used to cast me in parts that other casting directors couldn't imagine putting me in. Everything I was in, people were going crazy when I was onstage. I was the only one who got laughs. I do a fantastic take. I know what I'm doing onstage. And for me, to have that audience right in the palm of my hand is most satisfying. But to get up in front of a camera, I don't hear myself. Even when you run the tape over, it doesn't sound like me. I feel better about myself when I'm on the stage. Because I know that I can handle an audience. To me, the applause is more important than the bucks."

My mother proceeded to tell dozens of show business anecdotes, about a hammy coactor blocking her from the audience's view, or the very beautiful girl who was living with an Italian gangster and who couldn't tell her left foot from her right, or the curtain coming down at the wrong moment. She and her fellow troupers would get together to recount these stories and laugh and laugh, and we, her children, would sit there openmouthed, yawning. I still don't get the point of these vignettes. What was so funny about them? They were like war stories; I guess you had to have been there.

"When I toured with dinner theater, we used to have what we called the 'joyed-it' line. After the show, people would say, 'Oh I 'joyed it so much, how'd you ever get to learn all them lines? I 'joyed it.' And I used to say, 'Thank you very much' and shake hands with everyone on line. God forbid if I had a ring on my hand; I would die there. 'Thank you very much. Thank you very much.'

They were so busy talking, they never heard what I said. They would always want me to autograph their programs. I knew very well that they weren't going to hold onto those programs, when the car got dirty they would toss them. But my bio was in the program, and it was nice having them know that I had a little notoriety besides that show. When people recognized me back in the city, I loved it. And when it stopped, it was okay. Because if it had gone any further, then it would have been an annoyance. I went on Joe Franklin's program one night, and people saw it. They would say, 'I saw you on Joe Franklin's show.' It was fun. But I still would give up the whole thing to go on a good tour. You know, I gave it all up once to do *Fiddler on the Roof*. When I went away on tour with *Fiddler*, I made only a hundred dollars a week, which is ridiculous. Justin [her Tevya] and I each made a hundred dollars a week. No, wait, I made a hundred-and-ten because I was company manager, so I made an extra ten dollars a week. I had a lot of fun on that show. Oh God, that was fun! I also had fun on *The Reluctant Debutante*. That was a good tour. That was six months. See, when you go on tours like that—six months here, six months there—you don't need to have a separation. Who needs divorce; I was never home anyway? That's what I wished could have lasted."

"And it didn't because . . . ?"

"Well, one of the theaters burnt down. And one of them thought we were charging too much; they were losing money. And another one decided that he wanted to buy his own theater, and he was going to do his own producing. For different reasons, the whole production company fell apart. I really had a big disappointment last summer. Steffi got a company together, and I auditioned. And I went to see Steffi. When I got there, I found that the dance captain was someone who had been part of a company where I had worked in Canada. The producer had recommended me. The dance captain had recommended me. I got up there and I sang and I was not the least little bit nervous. My voice was absolutely perfect. The reason why he was considering me was because Maria Carnilova was not available. He was ready to call me, ready to sign the contract, when Maria Carnilova decided to make herself available. Now that's the second time it happened to me. The first time it happened, I went to Jay and I said I was very disappointed. He said, 'Don't be disappointed, don't be unhappy, because look at it this way: If someone came to me with the same talent that you have, and could fill the role the same way you could, and you both wanted the role, I would take you, because I know how you perform, I know how you take direction, I'm familiar with you. The same thing with them: they chose someone they had toured with before. You're an unknown quantity. And although I know what you can do, that director doesn't.' The producer called me, and he was very nice. He said he was delighted with my audition. But I didn't say, 'Call me again sometime.' It took the wind out of me. I didn't want to start again. If that had happened last year, with a year's tour and the money that was involved, I would have taken the old man and put him in a home right away. But the fact that it wasn't happening meant: let's forget about the whole thing."

## *The Obsession*

"I don't know. It seems like my whole life has been one series of blackmails after another. I felt that he blackmailed me into staying with him, and that changed my life; it was not fulfilled. I thought when you kids were old enough, I'd be able to get out of it. And when you were old enough for me to get out of it, he trapped me again! He had that fucking—phony stroke that wasn't even a stroke. But what the hell."

Needless to say, there was nothing phony about my father's stroke. It was genuinely incapacitating, and he never regained his full strength afterwards. I have no idea what might have been going through my mother's head when she put forth this strange assertion. I considered it at the very least a tribute to her fatalistic bookkeeping that she had managed to construe his illness as a mean-spirited stratagem, one in a long line of dirty tricks pulled on her, beginning with the death of her father, ensuring that she would somehow get the shitty end of the stick.

"It hurt that my life was not fulfilled. And that became an obsession. I guess it still is."

"An obsession to fulfill yourself?"

"Oh I'll never fulfill myself now. It's too late. I look at all those years that were wasted. Everything I've done after I was fifty years old should have been done in my late twenties and thirties."

"Well, what was your obsession?"

"The fact that I wasn't free, that I couldn't leave him. He trapped me and kept me down, and I wasn't permitted to do anything. I wasn't permitted to be a person. Looking back at it, I felt like I was being put in a big ocean of quicksand, and I couldn't get out of it. You know how frustrating that is? I couldn't get out of it until I was fifty years old. By that time my life was over. I won't say it's *over,* but I mean it's late. People retire when they're fifty years old. I was peaking at that time."

"But I don't understand: how can you be kept from being a person when you are a person?"

"The person I wanted to be. That I couldn't be."

"Describe that person."

"I wanted to leave him. I didn't want to live with him. I wanted to be able to see other men. I wanted to make choices of other men. I wanted to perhaps marry somebody else. And I couldn't! Because every time there was a possibility, every time I would get another job, I couldn't go out with another man. I couldn't do anything."

"But you did see other men."

"It was a very limited thing. It had to be limited. Because I was tied down also by my own sense of guilt and, I guess, morality. Strangely enough, I'm a very moral person."

"I agree."

"And that helped to undo me."

"Did you ever think that maybe it wasn't his blackmail, but your own cowardice? That had you taken his dare, you might have come out on top?"

"I took his dare, a couple of times. And I banged up against a brick wall. The first time I took his dare, he came back. The second time, he had a stroke. Every time, it was something else. And I guess

I was a bit of a coward too. I was afraid to face the world at that point."

"You had four kids to take care of—"

"Yeah, that was not an easy thing. But I still had a daycare center that could take care of them during the day. I had friends that were able to watch them in the evenings and late afternoons. There are ways to get around the problem. If I was able to do it, I would have done it. But when you come home from work, and climb up the stairs hauling two kids by the hand after you, at five o'clock at night, and find a man sitting in the kitchen on a rocking chair reading a newspaper, who doesn't say hello, but instead says, 'What have you got to eat?' it's tough to face. What kind of a greeting is that? What kind of relationship can you have with a man who doesn't acknowledge you as a person?"

"Let me ask you something. Did you ever think you might be giving too much energy to your hatred of him, and that that was getting in the way? In other words, what would have happened if you'd simply ignored him and said, 'I'm living in the same house with this man, but I'm not really his wife.'"

"I did that for a long time. As a matter of fact, we finally wound up in separate rooms. But it wasn't easy because we had a small apartment and a bunch of kids. I wasn't able to do that until we moved into Nostrand Avenue. In Nostrand Avenue I had my own room."

"Did you ever feel bitter against the kids, that we were holding you back from your freedom?"

"Yes. Because he said he would take you away from me. I couldn't blame you children, but I felt I had made a sacrifice for the children. And then I figured, they're going to grow up, they're not gonna know, they're not gonna care. They're going to live their own lives. And here I am with a rope around my neck, and they're not going to give a shit. There's no point in talking about it anymore; this is not useful."

"So you think that having this taped conversation is not useful? Why?"

"Because you are the only one listening. Does it really matter to you? You grew up; you have your own life. You're not going to do anything now to alleviate the situation, because there's nothing you can do."

"I can't alleviate *your* situation, but what I can do is something different from what you just claimed, that we don't care about the sacrifices you made. I'm saying that by having this kind of conversation, I am *trying* to understand that sacrifice. What more can I do?"

"But it's too late. That's the problem. Once the barn is burned, there's nothing you can do about it."

"But you said we wouldn't understand. Look, Ma, when I was growing up, it was perfectly obvious to me that both of you were trapped. I felt like it wasn't any bargain having kids, because we held both of you down in different ways. I felt sorry for both of you. I *always* felt sorry for both of you. I never felt: 'Eh, it's their problem.' If anything, growing up in that household we had to fight through to our own selfishness, because we were overwhelmed by the tragic frustration of our parents."

I had the sense that I had said something penetrating, something true for a change. Her reply suggests either she hadn't heard it, or couldn't acknowledge it.

"So everything's 'all right' now, because he's the only child, and he has me all to himself. He's okay. He's perfectly happy. He has no competition."

"But don't you think that when you went into show business you managed to get a little bit of the life you wanted to have?"

"Of course. I had to. I ran away."

"Well, that was heroic of you." I was reverting to the good, empathetic son.

"It only lasted a couple of years, and now I'm stuck again. I can't leave him alone in that house. I can't."

"It seems to me that the fact that you had other lovers, and the fact that you had a show business career, was a tribute to your vitality."

"That means my life is over."

Oy. No point in trying to flatter her. "No, it doesn't mean your life is over. If I were you, I'd get separated from Father at this point."

"I don't intend to leave my apartment. It's my apartment, I was in show business" [they lived in Manhattan Plaza Towers on West 42nd Street, a complex that had units subsidized for actors] "and I worked for it. I earned it. I want him out of here. I can't get him out. He doesn't make enough money on Social Security for me to ship him someplace where he can live like a human being. See, again I'm trapped by my own sense of pity, my own sense of decency, and my own sense of guilt."

"But what if the children contributed?"

"I can't burden you children with that. If Lenny was a very rich man, or you sold one of your books to the movies and made a million dollars, I'd say, 'Okay, no problem.' I would have absolutely no qualms in asking you. And you would have no hesitation in handing it over. The way things are, could I burden you with, say, fifty dollars a month or a hundred dollars a month—we'll say fifty dollars a month from each one of you? Joannie doesn't work steady, Betty Ann has to take a proofreading job that makes her eyes fall out of her head so she can keep a health care program—"

"Let me tell you something, Ma: If you want to live separate from Father, you'll find a way, and the easiest way would be to give up the apartment. There's got to come a time when you say, 'Okay, I'll live in a place that's inferior, but at least I'll have my freedom.'"

"Sign the apartment over to him, and find another place of my own?"

"Exactly."

"It's not so easy. I've already looked."

"There are eight million people in New York. There's got to be an apartment for you. I'm not saying it's easy. I'm just saying: At some point, if you want something, you have to go after it."

"I could have done that when I had an income. I don't have an income anymore. My income is less than a hundred dollars a week. I have to stay in Manhattan Plaza, because there at least the rent is subsidized, to accommodate my income. But if I were to leave here, where would I go? Could I find something on my Social Security check alone? It's ridiculous! And when I see pictures of these men living in miserable SROs, no matter how badly I want him out of here, even I couldn't do that to him. Not even to him. So again, I'm stuck. Whatever God had in mind for me, it's either a punishment for something I've done, or a test for something that's coming up. Maybe He's trying me out for something that's going to be a real wing-dinger in my next life."

At the time this discussion took place, my mother had already gotten her divorce but they were still living together, victims, in a sense of New York City's scarcity of affordable housing. I think in retrospect I was being disingenuous in encouraging her to separate from my father. I had always been secretly pleased that they had stayed together so long. My urging her to quit him had more to do with impatience at the predictable direction the conversation was taking. It always seemed to end up in a place where she was frustrated, stymied, thwarted. That sense of being stuck, at an impasse, made me uneasy. I began searching for practical ways to act to break the logjam. It's a classic pattern between men and women: the woman wants to express her feelings of discontent about a bad situation and the man offers up logical alternatives. When the bad situation happens to be the patriarchy, it's understandable that the woman will want to give full voice to her resentment about a problem which realistically does not appear to be going away any time soon, just as it's understandable that the man—patriarchy's surrogate—will try to circumvent the root of the problem by proposing stopgap remedies. It becomes a way of cutting off the conversation: like if someone starts complaining in detail about his health, you say, "You should really see a doctor about that," meaning, "Stop complaining, I can't take it anymore."

## *The Argument*

There was a tension, like an emotional standoff, between my mother and me. It partly resulted from my reserve: as an adult, any difficult patches I might be going through I kept to myself. I had no intention of sharing confidences about the women I was seeing or even the professional challenges I was facing. I had the wary sense that if I offered her any admission of weakness or anguish she would pounce on it like red meat. It would either please her avidity for gossip too much, or she might use it against me at a later time. No, I couldn't allow that. But it bothered me, this layer of frost between us, and so, three-quarters of the way through the taping sessions, I decided to bring up the problem.

"So when I was about thirteen, what was I like?"

"Well, then you became a typical Lopate. You drove the teachers in your Hebrew School crazy. You wouldn't believe anything that anyone told you."

"You once told me that you could handle me until the time when my vocabulary exceeded your own, after which I was a lost cause."

"Did I? I don't remember. I may have."

"At what point did you start to feel there was a distance between us, that we weren't as close as we once had been?"

"I don't know, I think it started when you went to college. Might have even been before. But when you got out of the house, I felt it was something that you had wanted very much. You were on a leash; you needed to get away from me. You said something which I felt I had to buy, because I had no choice. You said: 'I'm not leaving because I don't love you, I'm leaving because I'm afraid I might love you too much. And I don't want to be Frances Lopate's son, I want to be Phillip Lopate. I don't want to be an extension of you. I have to be my own person.' Part of that I buy. Part of it I think you said just to make me feel better. And that's when I felt, He's gone on and that's it."

"Did you feel that way with Lenny also?"

"No, I never felt that with Lenny."

"Why do you think that?"

"Because Lenny kept in close touch. Lenny is more—was always more affectionate. I felt close to him because he *was* closer, physically, emotionally. You wanted to be your own person. You became your own person. It wasn't just a blending in; it was something completely separate. I figured, that's the way you wanted it, that's the way it had to be. You never reached out to me, as Lenny did on occasion. You got married very young, and you went away for a long time, a year in Spain. You came back, and you were involved in your own life. When your divorce came, it was like reading about it in the newspaper. That's why there was a separation."

"I don't understand how I could have come to you with my problems when you had always seemed so troubled to me. Even when I was very young, you had come to me with your problems. Seriously, I felt that you were very self-absorbed. It might be flattering to you to come to you with my problems, but it didn't feel natural to me."

"It isn't always a matter of coming to me with problems. It could be the good things, the nice things. When you called me once every couple of weeks, with Lenny it was once every couple of days."

"I don't think it's true, though. In talking to Lenny, it's not the case. He doesn't call you so often."

"I'm talking about what was then, not now. Now it doesn't matter, I accept that, it's fine."

"But when he was twenty, twenty-one—?"

"Yes. And it wasn't only the frequency, it was the quality of the calls. You and I never had anything to say to each other. I'd get on the phone with him and yak yak yak yak yak for an hour. Of course Lenny could talk for an hour."

"Well Lenny is a man of the telephone—that's how he is, he lives by the telephone."

"I can talk to Betty Ann for an hour; I can talk to Joannie for an hour."

"No one can talk to me for an hour on the telephone. I like to get off very quickly and return to what I'm doing."

"But that's only an example. It's just metaphorically speaking."

"No, I think it's true. I have never been a great one for a certain kind of daily life. I can't spend time making small talk about my day and what happened next. I always have this 'back to work' feeling, you know? I'm driven."

"Okay. I understand that. Now I can accept it."

"This is not the full answer, but it wasn't personal. I do it with everyone."

"I'm talking about when you were nineteen. I'm not talking about now."

"No, but even when I was nineteen I didn't hang around much or chatter on the phone."

"All right, I just have to accept it because that's what happened. But you asked why I felt the separation, so I'm telling you why. You don't have to defend it, because it's not insulting anymore."

"It's interesting. I remember during those years I would come home for holidays, for family gatherings; it seemed to me that I was putting in my time. And you would have these long talks with me, when you would basically unburden yourself. Yet in spite of the fact that we continued to talk that way, you still didn't trust me. In other words, I continued to be your confidant, but not trusted on another level. There was a division. Even now—"

"I'm not even sure I used you as a confidant, I'm not too sure that I unburdened myself to you."

"You did, Mom. I remember when I wrote that first novel, *Best Friends,* which never got published, there was a long scene with the mother telling the son everything that was going on. That was taken from life. So a certain kind of interaction was happening . . . this interests me, because it seems this is happening again. We could have a series of fine conversations, and then at the end of it, you would go back to saying: 'You know, I just can't talk to Phillip. I don't know what it is but something in me chokes up.' In other words, you have a kind of amnesia, where you didn't remember that you *had* talked to me. We always go back to square one, which was the dramatic separation—my 'rejection' of you. You wouldn't incorporate a certain kind of contrary evidence."

"It depends on what I said to you, on what you consider by me 'unburdening' myself. I don't know what you mean by 'unburdening myself.'"

"I mean, you would tell me what was making you unhappy."

[Laughs] "How many times a week? We would never have had enough for those conversations at that time. Even now, I couldn't tell you what was making me unhappy, because *everything* makes me unhappy. You know, it isn't that I say I can't speak to you. It's just that sometimes I felt I couldn't get into details with you. I felt that our relationship was a very superficial one. It was never a very warm one. I always felt that you were—distant. That your interest was clinical. Grist for the mill. That it was going to go in a book. Now, in these conversations we've been taping you're interested in where you came from, so it's still just for you. It's you you're interested in—"

"This just shows what a past master you are at pooh-poohing things. . . . It started very early when I was five and you would say, 'Oh you're not kissing me because you love me, you're kissing me because you want a quarter for some ice cream.' And over the years, the ice cream, the book, whatever it is, you have a way of turning my interest in you into something that's not completely authentic. When you do that with a five year old kissing his mother, saying 'Mama, mama, mama,' and you turn to that kid and you say, 'You don't love me, you just want something out of me,' then that's just insecurity speaking. It's an insecurity that can no longer accept that the interest in you is authentic. And all I can say at that point is, 'Hell, I'm not going to get involved in that. That's just nuttiness.'"

"You were just admitting that a long conversation you wrote in a novel was based on a conversation that we had had. So what am I supposed to gather from you?"

"You're saying if I write about you, it means I'm not interested in you, I'm only interested in you as material—why the 'only?' That's the key word. I'm 'only' interested in you so that I can get something out of it. When I say I'm interested in my roots, you say, 'Aha! He's only interested so that he can find out about *his* roots.' It's a rhetorical figure. You reduce it so that it only becomes an 'only.' There's nothing else. There's no warmth; there's no interest that I have toward you. I mean, you *made* me, to a great extent: obviously I'm interested in you. Why else would I even be talking to you right now? But somehow you are a master at negating and reducing. My own affection is—it's like a reducing mirror: you turn it the other way and it shrinks. You do it so well, I admire you for it. But it's dumb! Anybody else might say: 'We've been having heart-to-heart talks all these years, so maybe it's not so superficial, this relationship. He's written about me a lot; maybe that means I'm on his mind.' [Pause] Do you have anything to say in rebuttal to this statement?"

"Your behavior seems to point up my argument. I realize that writers have to use what they learn from life. They have to use their own experiences, the people that they know, their families, the man on the street as characters, etcetera, etcetera. So naturally they're going to use their family."

"No, on the contrary, there are lots of writers who don't write about their families. If I write about my family it's because I'm engrossed by my family. It's had a terrific influence on my life. A writer is also a human being who wants to communicate. I'm not only writing to communicate with anonymous readers, I'm writing to communicate to you and the people I'm writing about. Obviously I'm trying to say things that somehow I've not been able to say. I was not able to say what I was really thinking and feeling. And by rejecting that idea, you can't take seriously my writing as a form of communication. If I am communicating, I'm communicating to you as well."

"I see what you're doing as using us."

"It's such a paradox: why would I be the only one who uses you, whereas the other children love you? What is it about me that doesn't love you but only uses you?"

"Well they have no other use for me, except for that."

"If I stopped writing tomorrow, that would be an act of love that would prove my interest in you? [She laughs] That's ridiculous. It can't be that just because I'm a writer, my mother suspects all of my interest in her."

"That's not what I meant and you know it."

"I don't really know what you mean. I would think that my interest in you has been proven again and again. Look, I'm someone who has achieved a certain amount. I have a lot to be proud of. Now, I very often think about my mother, I think about my father, I think about my family a great deal. Naturally it's going to get into my work. You could say: 'Gee, here's somebody who's achieved a certain amount, it's a tribute to a family that he cares about them so much he fills his art with them.' Why would that never occur to you?"

"Well, maybe you're right, maybe I am insecure. Maybe I have to latch onto some reasons. Maybe I feel I don't deserve it."

"No, *I* have an accusation, and it's that you don't understand the way I express love because you never have understood me very well. You see me as being clinical when I listen to you, when I'm paying attention. You don't see that when I am being quiet and paying attention—you put the worst face on it, the worst interpretation. You don't understand me very well. Other people understand that when I'm listening and paying attention, it's a tribute; it is how I give. You knew all along that I wasn't a really big talker, I'm the kind of person who observes. You knew my character. And yet, when I express my character, it comes out to you as clinical."

"Well, you asked me when I felt the division actually started. And I said it was when you said you wanted to go your way."

"Mmhm. And it must have hurt you a lot at that time. I see now that I hurt you, and to some degree intentionally. I wanted to push you away. And I take responsibility and blame for that. I don't think I was very nice to you."

"It was hard to take."

"You know, I was a teenage boy who was trying to establish his own identity. As I saw it, I was being driven crazy, and I . . . Somehow, you see me as this stony cold person, and I saw myself as having gone through the biggest crisis of my life in which I tried to kill myself. So you impute a kind of strength and rejecting power to me, which I didn't feel at the time. I felt I was fighting for my life. Lenny is a very dominating person; you're a very dominating person. Betty Ann is a shrill and hysterical person. I had to put some distance there. That made a whole lot of sense at the time. Even now when I come home, I feel like I can't get a word in edgewise at a family gathering. But I don't want to take back what I said: I do think that I hurt you with that, and I don't think it was—"

"If saving your life meant a complete rejection of your mother, if you had to, you had to."

"Not just my mother—"

"Your whole family. I'm not worrying about what they felt, right now I'm worrying about what I felt."

"I'm just saying it wasn't like: 'Hey, I'm so terrific and cool.' I was in a battle. It was life and death."

"It was difficult for me, too, when you tried to kill yourself. For one thing, I wasn't told about it until the next day. That wasn't right. I felt that I wasn't—needed."

"Well I was in a coma—"

"I wasn't talking about you. You know, it was wrong. All those things added up. It was wrong. The whole thing was wrong. And I was very angry. I felt—guilty. Any time a mother sees a son in a state like that, unless she's crazy she's going to feel guilty. And I felt guilty. There was nothing I could do to help you. And you sloughed it off."

"What do you mean, I sloughed it off?" I asked.

"When I asked you what would have happened if they didn't get to you in time, you said, 'I would have died.' Like it was no big deal."

"Yes, of course. But every person who tries to commit suicide has to have a certain fidelity to the act. They don't want to say, 'I was wrong, I was stupid.' They always say for a period of, say, two weeks, 'I'd do it again if I had the chance' or 'I don't regret it.' That's just pride. See, what I don't understand is, how come at that moment you were so suffused with guilt and with anger in the hospital that you couldn't see, here was a kid who was in trouble and who needed care and maternal love?"

"I was angry at myself, not at you!" she said.

"I think *you* pulled back at that moment."

"No, they wouldn't let me in to see you. They wouldn't even let me upstairs."

"And what happened when I got out of the hospital?"

"*You* wouldn't let me in. You told me not to come. That was it. And you wonder why I felt rejected? There was nothing I could do,

I was cut off. I figured, that's it. That's how you wanted it. I know, you were only seventeen years old, you were going through a painful time—"

"And also, I didn't feel like you were paying real attention to me. I was in agony, and you couldn't see it. The family couldn't see it. I had been the one who was voted in high school 'most likely to succeed.' I could not—partly because of my own craziness and partly because of other people's insensitivity to receive it—I could not get across the pain that was inside me. I could not make it be believed. The only way I could make it be believed finally was to try to kill myself."

"Yes, but when I wanted to come see you, you wouldn't let me."

"But I didn't really think that you knew who I was. Betty Ann was acting up: she got a lot of attention. Lenny was melodramatic and everyone listened. I felt like I was an invisible man. Nobody saw me in the family. It was like: 'Here's an engine that runs, nothing's wrong with it, so why fix it? Let it run and do not disturb it.'"

"But the engine took itself away from the family. That's the one thing you don't want to accept."

"I accept it, but I'm trying to say there was a reciprocal missed connection. I took myself away from the family partly because I felt the family could not see me or understand me. They didn't know what I was truly like . . . Well, that's a simple idea," I admitted.

"You're oversimplifying the whole thing anyway. Because when I wanted to reach out, you wouldn't let me."

"I—I think that's true. I really do. I didn't want you to."

"All right. So you wonder why I get the feeling that there's a separation. Because I have the feeling you *want* a separation. So all your protestations can't get through that barrier!"

"Okay. Now can we understand what *I'm* trying to say? I don't think you knew who I was. I don't think you were paying close attention. In other words, you did not take the trouble to find out what kind of person I was. Maybe I did not know how to act out in such a way that you, who were conditioned to recognize hysteria and a certain kind of colorful dramatic carrying on, could detect it."

"So?"

"So these things are interconnected. In other words, I felt rejected to begin with. I felt that I was not understood. I was not getting across. I had to find other people to get across to. In a wacky way, I sort of thought that Betty Ann *got* who I was, because we were very close at that time. But I didn't really feel that anyone else was paying attention, they were so wrapped up in their own problems. If I went to a friend, the friend could at least listen to me like for the first time. I could see that I wasn't getting across very well in the family. But it was reciprocal. I wasn't putting myself across accurately and the family wasn't taking the real trouble to see underneath."

"Many years later, when I said to you we could at least think of each other as friends, you said I don't need you as a friend. I got friends."

"I needed you as a mother."

"And yet, you rejected me as a mother. It was hard for me to know where I stood. So I just slipped away and waited until you were ready to make it known where I stand."

"I always thought that you were all too quick to react with hurt feelings, and not to react the way a mother should, which was with love and amusement to a child—"

"I could never react with amusement to you, Phillip. You were not an amusing person to me. I could never take you lightly."

"Why not?"

"Because—everything was always heavy with you."

[What did she mean by this? Why heavy, why this dark threnody? I like to be amused; I don't think of myself as so "heavy." Was it because, as I used to think, I had been her favorite, and then she felt pushed aside by me? Or was it some kind of static that occurred when the two of us got together, jamming the lighter waves?]

"I still have two letters of yours," she said, "stashed away deep down in a drawer, where no one's ever going to find them until I die."

"Those were written when I was in therapy and suddenly in touch with my anger against you."

"Yes. And I still remember how those letters tore me apart."

"You're a person with a long memory and the desire to hold grudges."

"It's not a question of a grudge. But every facet of our relationship has always been a heavy one. I can never take you lightly."

"Even when I was a child?" I asked.

"I'm talking about when you decided that enough was enough. And it had to be: goodbye. You were sweet, you were wonderful, you were good, you were adorable. And little by little you got older and decided that you didn't want to be my baby anymore. You left. I had no other way that I could think of you. I had one head, I was trying to divide it into six parts, and it's hard enough to keep it on one thought. And whoever got shortchanged—"

"But you knew enough that when it comes to adolescence, kids have to make a separation from their parents. So why didn't you just take it as a characteristic reaction in that period of my development?"

"Because of the way it was done. It was done in such a cold way that when I wanted to be friends with you, you kept rejecting me and rejecting any hand I put out to you. You just didn't want me! You made it known in no uncertain terms. Now I'm not a person who can take rejection lightly."

"But you don't seem to understand it developmentally. This was something I had to do at that time."

"Sure. But you know, I'm also a person, I was also developing at that point. I was going through a lot of developing, because I was at a difficult mental stage myself, which unfortunately I couldn't expect anyone else to understand because you were all young and I was young, mentally, with you."

"I know. The mother that I wanted and that I dreamed about would be a mother who would take me a little more lightly, who would not take to heart like an operatic soprano, some Madame Butterfly, this thing that to me I had to do to get on with my life. And who would say, 'Okay he's going through a stage, he's in therapy, let him rant and rave, big deal.' I always hoped for not only a little more lightness but a little more understanding."

"I did understand it. The way I understood it was rejection."

"Yeah, but that's not understanding. To see only the black and not the white is not understanding. To see my interest in you as only using you and never caring is myopic. It's a terrible nearsightedness. It's like when I say to you, 'Ma, tell me when you're sick or you've twisted your ankle, I want to know,' and you don't make the phone call and decide that I've rejected you. I mean, there's something strange here. No letters, no phone calls from you?"

"If you want a Jewish mother, Phillip, you're not going to get it from me."

"There's something in-between a hovering Jewish mother and a mother who says, 'Okay, you hurt me? That's it for the rest of your life.'"

"It isn't that you 'hurt' me and that's it for the rest of your life. It's that I *believe* you when you say, 'Don't.'"

"You believed that once because you wanted to hear it so much. You never believed all the other things that I said. You don't believe it today. I say to you, 'I'm interested in you; I care about you. Ma, if you're having a slipped disc, I want to know. I'll take you to the hospital. You can depend on me, you can lean on me, if you need to move something, I'll be happy to move it.' In one ear and out the other. No belief. This is a person who only wants to hear one kind of statement! How is it that, according to you, I tell the truth sometimes, and other times I lie so much? Why would I want to lie all the other times?"

"When do you tell the truth?"

"Well, you say I tell the truth when I reject you. I don't tell the truth when I don't reject you. [She laughs] It's as simple as that. Never could it be more clearly stated. That's what I've learned from you: The truth is rejection. Love is not the truth."

"I don't know why. I don't know why I've always felt a certain coldness from you."

"Maybe it's in yourself. Maybe you have a coldness toward me."

"I never thought I did. In fact I always thought that you were the one—"

"There's got to be some coldness where there's this remoteness, no?"

"I've always felt you were cold and remote. I always felt that you preferred it that way."

"And you don't want to take responsibility for your own part in this distance?"

"I felt that I was reacting. I felt that you were acting, and I was reacting to your feelings."

"You know, it's wonderful, Mom, even though you are more than twenty-five years older than me to begin with, and you were on this planet a much longer time, you have always just *reacted* to me. You were never the initiator."

"That's the way I felt."

"Bottom line: 'That's the way I felt.' No new information or insight can enter. 'I felt that I was reacting to you.'"

"You're overlooking something. You're overlooking a past tense. You're not accepting the fact that I'm leaving myself open to development. That's not a hole in my head. That's an open mind."

"That's good."

"I pride myself on an open mind. I've never been together with you this many times in the last fifteen years. I never got your side of it, and I don't think you ever got mine."

"I got the side of your feelings toward me, but I never got the side of your whole life. And there's so much in it that is stunning and amazing."

"It's not stunning and amazing, it's just an ordinary normal life. But I feel that I have options for our future. You can either take it or leave it. I can either like you, or love you. Or both. I've always liked you. And always loved you. I was always afraid to show it. Because I was afraid you would reject me."

"You know that point when a seventeen-year-old boy doesn't want to kiss his mother on the lips?"

"I was not going to soul-kiss you. [Both laugh] I don't soul-kiss anybody."

"I was threatened. I had to pull away physically."

"I meant emotionally pull away."

"There's no question that I emotionally pulled away. I felt the whole thing was a vortex, a terrifying vortex that was very dark.

And the peculiar thing is that I moved away before I tried to kill myself. I couldn't differentiate between the darkness in myself and the darkness outside of myself. At a certain point I just sort of needed to put it on the family as a defense, but obviously there was a lot of darkness in me. All of that achievement-orientation fed into 'You're nothing unless you achieve.' I never felt like you pushed us to get good grades. I felt you were saying that it was okay, you don't need to excel always. You told us that all the time. I did feel from Father that intellect was the only worthwhile thing in the world. I had to get Lenny to play ball with me—I couldn't get that from Father, because his whole sense of self-worth was bound up with bragging about what he knew. Father would criticize someone in the hospital for using a double negative. Here's a guy who's almost dying and he's priding himself on good grammar."

"So many people I know have kind hearts, they try. I . . . I'm an intellectual snob. But there are times I realize that it's not necessary. You lose a lot of friends that way."

So the argument wound down. We had duked it out, thrown as many direct jabs as we could, and now we were smoothing over the conflict, her by saying she was open to future change, I by shifting my reproach to my father. It had been almost impossible to disentangle our separate narcissisms: which one was more self-absorbed than the other. There were moments in the discussion when I had a heady, exciting sense of trying to tell the truth, finally, about the two of us. But there was also something ridiculous about my attempt to convince her by logic, like a Cartesian proof, that I loved her. Underneath it all, I thought: 'She's right, I've not been loving enough toward her, I have kept my mother at arm's length.' All defensiveness aside, I think I have to acknowledge that I am not the warmest person in general, and I try to compensate for that chilly detachment by showing interest, concern, professional generosity, kindness, and humor, which tends to work better for students or friends, with whom the interactions are briefer and more infrequent than in family life. What I could never get my mother to understand was that if I could not be as warmly affectionate with her as she craved, that did not negate in any way my desire to help her, to stay in touch with her, to check in from time to time and see how she was doing. If she mistook this interest of mine as clinical or literary or insincere or merely the enactment of filial duty, that was a pity. I was quite fascinated by her, as you might be of a tiger who could maul you at any moment, but who could also strike you as touching and noble.

Something more should be said about that accusation of mine that I had been badly misunderstood, which now strikes me as petulant. Who isn't misunderstood by his family? By the time this argument took place, almost twenty-five years after my teenage suicide attempt, I was so well over the state of mind propelling me toward that self-destructive act that I could barely identify the person who did it. And now he seems to me a complete stranger. No doubt I was trying to turn the tables on my mother, shifting the taped discussion defensively from her complaint that I had rejected her to my lament that she had failed to see I was in trouble. The one live ember, the one aspect of my relations with others (not just my family) that had continued to distress me, was that people saw me as so calm, contented, and on an even keel, that they could not perceive my sadness. But whose fault was that? From the time I was in high school I had developed a façade of equilibrium as much out of stubborn pride as stoicism, neither wanting to belabor others with my inner turmoil nor having the dramatic flair to do so. And it worked, by and large, convincing me, once I had gotten that suicide attempt out of the way, that I was doing all right. What mattered to me most was to be productive, and it was through writing that I could also express some of my lingering sadness. I've always suspected that many writers who come from large families are the observers, the ones who don't dominate the dinner table but wait to have their say when they are alone in their study.

But it's also true that writers do blithely use the people around them as material, in ways that hurt, that baffle those they write about, regardless of how much a nonwriter may grasp the intellectual argument for that freedom. Czeslaw Milosz, the great Polish poet, said something to the effect that when a writer is born into a family, that family is finished. I saw in the end why my mother mistrusted me, and why she had every right to resent my having written about her. Maybe I had staged this whole set of interviews just to get to the bottom of our mutual mistrust. If so, I had been only partially successful.

## *My Brother Becomes the Bad Guy*

"How are you today?" I asked, at the beginning of the next taping session.

"How could I be? My son hates me, my daughter-in-law hates me. And you don't want to get in the middle of it."

"What is it? Tell me the story. I'm at a loss to know what's going on."

"Lenny and Theresa [his wife at the time] invited Pop for dinner. Okay. It's a pleasure when he goes away. You know how I feel when he goes out of the house; I enjoy it. I have my time to myself. But it started to pour. They wanted me to come and pick him up. Lenny called me, said they couldn't get a cab. And I said no."

"They couldn't get a cab? That sounds like they had good reason to call. How else was he supposed to get home?"

"The same way he got there, by public transportation. They could have called a car service. And they could have kept him overnight if they were that concerned. I mean, I had a big beef with my sister years ago. In 1938 she sent me out in the biggest hurricane they ever had in New York. And I never forgave her and I never forgot it. You don't turn someone out in the pouring rain. My car will not work in the rain. They know it. Why should I go out and get stuck in the middle of the city in the pouring rain, have to call the Triple A, and start with that cab nonsense all over again?"

"And what did they say?"

"They were very—stiff. That is the only way I can describe it. Theresa did call again and say that he was on his way home. But she was very stiff. What else can I say? I don't want to be responsible. They have no idea what it means to have to do for, and pick up after, and clean up after someone whom you don't like, every single day of your life. And every day it's getting harder and harder.

It's not something I do out of a sense of love, and I think it's wrong that I should have to do for someone I don't love. They were saying he was going to get mugged. He didn't get mugged!"

"Well, it's understandable they said that: he presents a kind of frail target for muggers—"

"He doesn't present as frail to the world as he does to his family. You see, that's what they will not accept, because they don't see it and they don't believe it. They don't know what a fraud he is. I see it. I watched him out the window and I saw him walking down the street. He practically skipped down the street! He was strong. He had a sense of purpose, and he walked like he knew where he was going."

"What happened then?"

"He came home!"

"So the real principle that should be established from this is that—" I was about to say something along the lines of alternate plans should be put in place next time, when she finished the sentence for me.

"Is: Leave me alone. *Leave me alone.* If he lived in somebody else's house, you wouldn't call me to go and do it. I'm divorced from him. I'm not his wife. There are very few advantages that I have gotten from that divorce. Number one: I absolutely refused to give him an enema when he got his physical, and I had been doing that for him for years. I don't want to do it anymore. It goes against my grain and it's wrong for me to have to do it. Now I refuse to clip his beard. I think Lenny should have to do that. Lenny's an expert and he knows just how the beard should look. I shouldn't have to do that. It's too personal and I don't want to do it. And number three, I don't want to have to be responsible for his comings and goings. If Lenny wants to entertain him, take him out during the day and send him home during the day. Or if he's going to take him out at night, see that he gets home. Don't depend on me! I am no longer his keeper."

"So actually, something good could have come out of this, if they now realize they have to return him to the house. That's a valid principle." [This was me being desperate to divert her bottomless aggrievedness to something more practical.]

"I didn't discuss it with them. I don't think they're going to realize that. They are just going to stay angry. And I'm so mad because of what he said on his radio show."

"What happened with Lenny on the radio? I don't understand."

"His guest was describing his family, and Lenny said something like: 'You must have had a wonderful mother to have that sort of attitude toward them. I had a terrible mother.' Then he said, "Uh-oh, I shouldn't say things like that, because she might be listening. You never know, she sometimes listens. I mean, she gave us a lot of *looove.*" He tried to cover it over. But he doesn't know when I listen, because I don't tell him. That was pretty shitty."

"I can't believe you're not going to tell him that you heard him."

"Why should I tell him? Because he doesn't know, let him sweat it out."

"But he can't even apologize if he doesn't know—"

"He doesn't have to apologize. The first thing out of his mouth was he had a terrible mother. There's nothing to apologize for. You can't apologize for your attitudes and your thoughts. You can only apologize for an action."

"You actually think that's true, that he thinks that?"

"He must. Why would he say it to a perfect stranger out of the clear blue sky?"

"Well, he says lots of things. But last week you were telling me that you felt closer to Lenny than you did to me because he was much more caring—he called you up and everything."

"Now I know what a phony he is. It helps to know what people say behind your back. What you say in front of your face is one thing, but it's nice to know what people say behind your back."

"Not that it necessarily means he's phony, probably just that he's ambivalent."

"It's a form of phoniness."

"If you have two minds about somebody, then that's phony?"

"Two minds means two-faced."

"You never have two minds about someone? Like your friends or the people you perform with?"

"We're not talking about an acquaintance; we're not talking about someone in the workplace, or a neighbor. We're talking about someone a whole lot more important in your life."

"Okay. Let me give you an example: Betty Ann. It seems like you have had classically two minds toward her for years. On the one hand, you're very, very close to her, maybe closer than to any of your kids. On the other hand, you have a lot of doubts and criticisms about her. So don't you think you're of two minds about her?"

"I don't know. I don't think I do. I feel that she needs me more, so I have to give her more. I don't know what her feeling is toward me, but I'm starting to wonder from what Lenny said. Because that was the first thing—he didn't even hesitate, it popped right out like it was at the top of his head."

"If you don't tell Lenny, what is my role in this? Am I supposed to not tell?"

"No, you don't have to say anything. You said you don't want to get in the middle of it, so you're not. I'm just telling you. I'm getting it off my chest."

I was quite happy to have the onus of Bad Son shifted from me to my brother, for a change, though I knew it was only a matter of time before it shifted back. In the end, we would share the crown of recrimination.

To me—maybe to no one else—there is something grimly comic in my younger self's efforts to steer my mother away from Old Testament vengefulness or Manichean judgments toward forgiveness, toward accepting the inescapable ambivalence that may exist between loved ones. Ever the pedagogue, I kept clinging to the hope that she was not too old to learn these novelistic complexities about human character, and that I was the one to impart them to her. I was also arguing on my own behalf: If she could be made to acknowledge that human beings are impure mixtures of love-hate, attraction-repulsion, and other polarities, she could eventually realize that I did love her, in my conflicted way. She might even come to terms with her undesired pity for my father. I think she knew all of this, on some level, and would even wisely concur with it for limited periods of time, before relapsing to the black-and-white grudges of old.

## *Strays*

In the years when she went on the road with regional theater productions of *Fiddler on the Roof* or *The Boy Friend,* she would bring home young cast members, often sweet, sexually confused—"strays," we called them—and we were always nonplussed by the way these adopted children regarded her as their ideal mother, while we, her actual children, felt much more testy about her maternal record. Of course, it is often easier to be a surrogate parent for other people's children than one's own: the very stringency with which your progeny judges you is incentive enough to prove you can do it capably for a less biased audience.

I asked my mother about her tendency to invite sailors to our house for Passover services, or to let women whose husbands had beaten them live with us for weeks, even when we were quite poor. Or girls whose parents were giving them a hard time. Such was Vicky, a thoughtful young African American woman who went on to become an official in the American Communist Party. "I never quite understood Vicky's relationship to our family."

"Vicky was one of Joannie's friends from high school. She was having problems with her mother. Her mother tried to have her committed, saying she was crazy. Her mother was the one that was nuts. Just because a girl doesn't agree with her mother, doesn't mean she's crazy."

"If that were the case, we'd all be committed."

"That's for damn sure. I had a spare room, and Vicky moved in. It was all right. But after a while, I really didn't feel I wanted an extra daughter in the house. I thought it would be nice to be alone. I went on tour, and one of the girls in the show wanted to come home with me. I wrote to Vicky and said that this girl was coming back from the tour—I think it was *The Boy Friend.* I told her I would like to have the room back for my guest. So she moved out. When I think of it, it was cruel. But if I didn't, she'd still be there. She learned how to get along with her mother eventually."

"She interested Father a little bit. I got that impression."

"Father was dying to get into her. But he had a lot of competition because Lenny got into her. Lenny made time with lots of people that we didn't expect. But I could just see the old man, in his inadequate bumbling way, thinking that because she was young, and black, she was going to say okay. He had a lot to learn, that old fucker. But she still calls. She keeps in touch."

"I think it shows remarkable generosity on your part, to have taken her in in the first place."

"How could you say no to people in need? *If* they're really in need. That's the dichotomy I don't understand about myself. I always say, 'I could never hurt anyone who hadn't hurt me.' Then I think of the terrible things I say to your father, and I say some awful things to him, and he sits there and says: 'I wish I was dead.' And I say: 'That makes two of us; we both wish you were dead.' How could I say that to a human being—unless he'd hurt me first? I would never say it to anybody else."

"But doesn't it mean that you have a kind of loophole in your morality, which is the Reaction Loophole? As long as you could feel that you're reacting, that someone hurt you first, you can get away with almost anything. You no longer have any ethical standards as long as you perceive that somebody hurt you first."

"I'm simply reacting. I don't act first. I don't hit first. I don't push the first button. Someone's going to push that first button first, but it's not going to be me."

"So you never really felt that even though someone may have hurt you in the past, that didn't give you a license to keep hurting them in the future?"

"I sometimes forgive. I don't always forget, but I forgive. I keep calling my sister—she's so far out of it, she's in a hospital, she doesn't even remember that I called her the day before."

"I don't mean to imply that I'm any more moral than you are, Mom. Quite the contrary. It just seemed like a logical loophole in your system."

"It's not a loophole. I think it's a perfectly logical thing to do. I'm not Jesus. I do not turn the other cheek. I'm not a saint; I've never claimed to be. I don't see any reason why, if somebody hurts me, I should not hurt back. There's no reason not to, if I can."

"Okay. Let's agree to disagree."

"Then what's your sense of morality? Do you think it's all okay?"

"No, my sense of morality is, it's possible that I would hurt those people back. But a) it wouldn't necessarily make me feel justified to do it, and b) I wouldn't feel that I had a license to keep hurting them again and again, just because they had once hurt me."

"That's not the point, you see. My father used to say: 'The first time you hurt me, I'll react nicely. The second time you hurt me, I'll react nicely. The third time, you're going to get it.' All right? He would say it in German. So once *mit guten, svei mit guten, drei mit basen*. That's the thing: I will not hit back right away. If a person keeps hurting me, I find I'm justified to keep hurting back."

"It sounds like an intimidating policy."

"Speaking of intimidating, I'm surprised by how many people can be intimidated by me. I invited someone to my house one time that I worked with. He was a Greek actor, and I wanted him to get together with Kitty Moranis. I don't know if you remember her; she's a Greek actress. He knew her slightly and she knew him slightly. He was afraid that he would come into a home that would be intimidating. Do I give that kind of impression to people that I'm intimidating? Are people afraid of me?"

"Well, since you often have a sarcastic tone, and not everybody is equally sarcastic, some people are afraid of you, because they know that you can cut them to ribbons."

"I never think of anything nasty to say until it's too late."

"That's not so. You can be quite sarcastic in the moment."

"And yet my friend Helen tells me that she thinks of me as her role model. If I'm so sarcastic, how can I be someone's role model?"

What does one thing have to do with the other? I wanted to say. And: who is this Helen, another one of your lapdogs? Fortunately I kept my mouth shut. In retrospect I am in awe of her quick ability to sidestep criticism. Apparently she liked the idea of being thought intimidating, but not if it invited a critique of her as sarcastic. A good son would have figured out a way to flatter her charisma yet reassure her.

## *I Vant To Be Alone!*

I can remember times when my mother would say: "That's it! Enough! I can't take it anymore," and storm out of the house and not return for twenty-four hours. I had always assumed she staged these meltdowns so that she could have an excuse to visit a lover, but it seems I was wrong, as I found out when I asked her about them.

"Many times, believe me, I ran away from home," she said. "I would get into the car and go. I had a favorite place that I would sneak away to, all by myself. I would go to Orient Point. It was a wonderful place to go when you didn't want anyone to know where you are. I'd go there in off-season. There was a motel there that I would go to, even in the wintertime. It was nice, pleasant, warm and cozy, and I could just curl up by myself in bed and watch television and not care if there was dinner made or laundry to be done, nobody calling me or asking me or dragging and pulling on me or making demands on me. I always felt that there were demands being made on me: by children when they were small, and as soon as they were old enough not to make demands, he got sick and *he* made demands. All my adult life, there was always somebody making demands. Not leaving me alone, not giving me any solitude. I love solitude. Leave me alone! I had to get away. And he didn't understand that. No one ever really understood that. I always felt that I would love to be loved. Not *needed,* not for any other reason, not because I'm a mother or a wife, just because I'm *me.* And it never worked."

This was the second time I had heard this lament, of wanting to be loved without any expectations, like the lilies of the field. The first time I had let it pass without commenting; this time, no.

"Well it didn't work because it's unreasonable, because love always involves demands," I objected. "Some people would even say the whole process of becoming mature is accepting and growing from demands that are put on you. Demands are what make you into a person."

"But there never was a limit. There was never a give and take. I was always required to *give.* And I never got—I won't say never: I got back, at least partially for my service to my children, I got back love. And that's all I ever really wanted. There was never anything else I needed from you. But I never got anything that I really wanted from—my husband. He was supposed to be the biggest part of my life. He was supposed to be my crutch; he was supposed to be my helpmate. He was supposed to be a half of me, half of everything I think and do and want and feel. And he was never there. No, absolutely never. From the word go."

"About Orient Point: what was out there?"

"If I got there early enough in the morning, I'd park the car for all-day parking and get on a ferry that went across the Sound to New London. It was a long, long ride, and in the winter, a very rough ride. It's like going across the ocean—it *is* partly the ocean, at the very tip of Long Island. You know how Long Island is a fish tail? The bottom part of the tail is Montauk and the top part of the northern end is Orient.

"From that point, you can travel across the ocean to New London. It would be a couple of hours' trip, and then I would turn around and come back. The whole day was taken up with an ocean voyage. It was cold, always cold, even in the summertime. I'd get up on the top deck of the ferry and look down at the cabs of the trucks where the driver sits. There are a million dials they have to concentrate on in those eighteen-wheelers. And then I'd get in the car and drive to my favorite motel. I'd stay there overnight, and leave only when I absolutely had to. Then I'd drive back through Long Island, stop for somewhere to eat. I came back when I felt like it. I was relaxed. But I knew when I got back it would be the same nonsense, the same shit again."

"What did you think about when you were on the boat?"

"How wonderful it was to be free."

"And yet at the point when you could have left him, you didn't."

She paused for a moment. "Well, I thought it would go on forever, the touring. Then unfortunately, a couple of theaters closed down, Jay gave up the production company, and I had to start hustling. Then Daddy got sick again. He had to go to the hospital for three months; that was fairly recently, sometime in the last six years. There was nothing I could do. I was stuck. I couldn't travel anymore. But I did. I went away. I went to do a show in Padukah, Kentucky. I stayed there a little over a month. But the girls were saying, 'Ma, he's impossible. I don't know what to do with him. He won't go out. The house is getting to be a mess.' I told them to put him on a plane to Kentucky, where I was working. But I couldn't go traveling with him. Nobody would hire me to go on the road with him, and I couldn't leave him home."

## *Back to School*

"One day I was taking a walk. I'd been told, 'If you don't do something and get out of the house, you're going to go crazy. You're going to wind up in the loony bin. You got to get away from your husband at least two, three hours a day.' Mike, my therapist, even said to me: 'Take walks. Get out of the house and walk.' I was walking one day, and I noticed there was a school on the next block. I went over to the school—it was a New York City community college—and before I knew it I was up on the sixth floor and enrolling. I got so involved. For me it was one of the happiest times. I was going to school a couple of hours a day, and I was *good*. I was smart. I was saying to myself, 'This is the one who was stupid in school.' I loved it. I was able to reason, better than I was ever able to reason before. The only remedial course I had to take was math, because I never got as far as algebra before. I took the remedial in algebra, passed very, very high, and I was on my way. The only teacher that resented me, strangely enough, was my Psych teacher. Because I would sit there and wait for someone to answer his question, and when nobody would answer, I would raise my hand because I knew all the answers. I think he wanted to answer the question. After a while, I realized that I was antagonizing him by answering the questions, so I stopped. When it came time for the exam, I was ready, but he absolutely refused to give me an A. He gave me an A-."

It was at this community college that my mother also took several creative writing courses. She subscribed to *Writer's Digest*, that periodical for the ever-hopeful amateur, and had the pleasure of being told by one of her instructors that she was a better writer than her big-shot son Phillip. Creative writing teachers often see part of their job as being supportive morale boosters, and I can just imagine this woman sympathizing with my elderly mother against the Establishment literary world, as represented by myself.

So one part of the old childhood wound was salved. It was official: my mother was intelligent. (She was the only one who ever doubted it.) She eventually graduated with an Associate BA degree, which included a certificate she had earned taking courses in caring for disabled children. I attended her graduation, a lively affair in which many middle-aged women, mostly black and Hispanic, clomped onto the stage in high heels to receive their diplomas and flash a V-sign to their adoring families in the audience.

## *Trying to Sum up*

"I don't know, sometimes I think it's been a very wasted life, and sometimes I think it hasn't been."

"Well it sounds like both. It sounds like you accomplished a lot. You know, all your stories about show business, they're thrilling, in a way."

"I think what I did was out of desperation. It should have been done long before. It's what I wanted to do so badly. I'm just glad that I was able to do what I did, in the few years that I did it. So part of my life wasn't wasted. But what bothers me is all those long years before that *were* wasted. I remember standing by the piano; I was only a little kid. I think I must have been maybe about twelve, thirteen years old. It was in Mary's house. She was playing, and I was singing some popular song, and her husband Moe said, 'Honey, when you go into show business, I want to be your agent or your manager. Because I know you could really go places.' I never did."

"So do you want to go back on stage now?"

"I would like to go back onstage, but I don't want to have to travel. I don't know what to do with Daddy. But don't ever be surprised, once you're back in Houston, if you get a call from the airport. I might be waiting there with a suitcase."

"I would think that you'd still be able to travel and leave Father sometimes."

"I can't. I can't trust him alone in the house."

"But when you went to Egypt, for instance?"

"Okay, I went for two weeks. I came back and I never saw so many cockroaches in my life. He poured out his soups on the counter, and there was one beef spill on top of another beef spill on top of another beef spill, a big pileup of gook."

"Obviously, you would have to hire help to look after him."

"I'm not going to, because it doesn't pay. I hate to tell you a thing like this, but I did three weeks' worth of laundry the other day. There was one pair of socks and two sets of underwear. All right? Now you tell me how a man can live like that. The only time he changes is if I tell him to. And yesterday he stood on line for almost two hours waiting for about five pounds of cheese and two pounds of butter, and he had to pee, and he did. In his pants. And today, I had to say to him, 'Don't you think you ought to change your underwear?' If someone doesn't watch him—I know what happened in those two weeks when I was away. So I can't have anybody take care of him. And the girls don't want to get that close to him. They shouldn't have to."

"So I think the solution *would* be to put him in a home at this point."

"Yes. But the thing is, this is not something that's new. He's always been a slob. I told you at the beginning of our conversations about running a bath that he never took."

"If you've got a good pair of underwear, why change something that works?"

"That's funny. Anyhow, maybe I would try a showcase in New York again. But actually, I don't have much energy left. Unfortunately, I have a lot of physical ailments, which I don't kvetch about, but I know my limitations. I can't be on my feet too much. I found that out when I was traveling in Egypt. When they started walking through a big temple, I would have to stop, because my leg was numb. I did have that injured disc with the injured nerve, and my leg was paralyzed for four months, and I'm afraid now. I don't want to push it. I don't have the energy. I go shlep over to shop at Pathmark: if I do too much, I'm exhausted. I'm not half the girl I used to be. I have to face that now. So as much as I might want to—"

"What are your ailments?"

"I have the kind of arthritis that, even though exercise and walking are good for it, it has to be limited. I'm not even counting the diabetes and the high blood pressure, things like that. What bothers me most is the arthritis and the pain in the back. That really hurts me."

•

Not long after the taped interviews concluded, my mother put my father in a senior citizen's residence. We, the kids, were all behind her decision. She boasted that at the intake interview, the director thought she was Albert's daughter, not his wife. The senior residence was out in Far Rockaway, over an hour and a half away by subway, which meant that it was inconvenient to visit him, and it was also in a residential area blocks away from the commercial strip that contained a newsstand or barber shop, which inconvenienced my father, a passionate reader of newspapers. He also did not get along well with his roommate, an Orthodox Jew who barely spoke English. The very fact that he had to have a roommate spoke to a key problem with such institutional settings: downward mobility. Having clawed his way into the bottom rung of the middle class after a lifetime of toil, he was suddenly forced to descend to a lower station in life. Subsequently, my brother found him a spot in a genteel, top-of-the-line senior residence in the Lincoln Center area. But when his health began to deteriorate—and more importantly, his continence—they kicked him out and he was placed in a depressing nursing home in Washington Heights. There he hung on for a few years, before falling ill and dying of pneumonia in 1994.

There was little grief expressed by my family at his passing, but I insisted a few days after his death that we all get together and at least talk about him. True to form, my siblings had sardonic recollections. They certainly did not give in to sentimentality; nor did I, for that matter, though I was less disparaging about him and more insistent on the value of his intellectual bequests and his having labored to support us. To my surprise, my mother took me aside afterward and expressed a touching gratitude for my honoring him this way. "He was so intelligent," she said, "it was such a pity he didn't do more with his brains."

For her part, living alone suited her. She continued to work a series of jobs, first at a daycare center, then for a retired millionaire businessman whose accounts she helped keep up-to-date. She had a few last beaux, including one younger cousin: you had to hand it to her; she was a pistol. Not that these dalliances ever mellowed her. She continued to hold grudges and remained a narcissist of the first order. When I, having fallen in love with Cheryl, proposed to her, I waited a day to tell my mother the news, and when she found out that Cheryl's mother had already been told she was furious. At a lunch date between the two of them, my mother began listing all my crimes and flaws when Cheryl cut her off by saying, "Listen, Fran, I love your son and I don't want to hear you putting him down anymore." That seemed to give her pause. Nevertheless, at our wedding, just as the rabbi began the ceremony, my mother pushed noisily to the front of the room (you can see it on the wedding tape: suddenly the camera's view of the *chupa* is blocked by this large woman advancing like a boat in the foreground), complaining that she had not been given a seat commensurate with her importance as the mother of the groom. That was Mom.

In her final years she joined a group of old troupers who performed at senior citizens' homes. They were game, plucky show-business types doing hoary comedy routines and musical numbers. My mother had a few solos: I remember her plangent, effectively melancholy rendition of "I'm in a New York State of Mind." I saw the troupe perform several times, including once at a Chinatown community center where the Asian elders sat patiently in wheelchairs, some drooling and most not knowing what the fuck any of the English lyrics meant, but smilingly appreciative of the melodies and the attention from outside. My mother got a kick out of her fellow performers, their quirks and talents—like Ike, the near-blind black guitar player. Eventually the troupe even got around to performing at the senior community center in my neighborhood. I brought my daughter Lily, who was then around four, and Anthony, the boy her age next door, to the performance. When my mother launched into one of her solos, Lily and Anthony got up and began dancing around the ballroom floor. Everyone ooh'd and aah'd, thinking it was so cute, but my mother (never the most doting of grandmothers) was pissed off by this distraction from her performance.

Her ailments piled up; diabetes was a big concern, because she had to administer daily injections and would sometimes get the dosage wrong. My sister Betty Ann, by then a trained nurse, would come by and administer her shots whenever possible: she thought my mother might be playing Russian roulette with her medicine, flirting with suicide. Frances had always had a self-destructive bent, simultaneous with a powerful life force. Who can understand, not I, how these two opposing drives operated in tandem on her character? In any case, it was getting harder for her to move around the city, and she decided to quit the singing troupe.

She gave her last performance on a Friday. The next day, Saturday, she had a massive heart attack and died. Here is the part that makes me cringe: apparently the heart attack had occurred sometime mid-morning, and she lay on the floor for hours, not caring to or able to get to the phone and ask for help. Around five o'clock she phoned my sister, who lived in the neighborhood, and told her to come right away. Betty Ann called an ambulance and rushed over. As they were wheeling her out of the building, Manhattan Plaza Towers, on the way to Roosevelt Hospital, she expired. Or maybe not: maybe she was still alive when she got to the hospital and died there, before they could resuscitate her. I got the phone call—Cheryl and I were just getting ready to leave for a dinner party—and we sped to Roosevelt Hospital as fast as we could. There I saw my mother's body, still lying on the gurney in the hospital corridor. She looked bad, like—dead meat. She looked like a corpse, I guess. What are corpses supposed to look like? She looked quite uncomfortable, her belly's girth rising from the sheets like some foreshortened Renaissance painting, Mantegna's *The Dead Christ,* say, and the expression on her face was, as far as I could make out, dismayed. I wish I did not have to have that image always in my mind of my mother on the gurney.

# *Epilogue*

Above and beyond any attempt to reach the truth, I know that transcribing these tapes and writing my responses to them has been an attempt to keep my mother "alive" for as long as possible, to get her off the gurney, to hear her voice again, and, in this way, to bring her back to life.

So, in a strange way, we have come full circle: I began by telling about my mother's futile effort to call out to her father so forcefully as to deter him from passing into the shades, and now here I've been doing much the same thing, trying to summon her back from the underworld, largely by quoting her, with the quixotic hope that she will be pleased enough by the sound of her voice to re-emerge, however fleetingly.

Hearing these tapes again was a shock. Her voice filled the room where I write, just as strong and confident as it had always been. At times the things she said were so shocking, I would have to pause the tape and sit there, gasping. Uncle Morris? Really? And when it came to the argument near the end, when I tried to convince her that I did love and care about her, I was flabbergasted, sweating, as though I were still defending my life. Her voice was the original Other, but it was also a part of me. As a baby I had first learned human speech from listening to her, and as a child I had internalized that voice to such an extent that it was hard to say where she left off and my own voice began. That writing voice from which I take dictation, and of which I am so proud, started out being hers. (I still hear her in my head, sixteen years after her death. I don't hear my father anymore because he was so silent, but when I look in the mirror I see him, especially when I don't smile—that same grim, stern expression.)

Listening to and transcribing these tapes, I was impressed by the sweep of my mother's life—all this woman had gone through. Born to European immigrants into a comfortable middle-class home, she was her parents' favorite but lost them at such an early age. She was raised by strict, indifferent siblings, a runaway and high school dropout. She was forced to reinvent herself over and over: working at a beauty parlor, becoming a housewife and a mother, running a candy store, working in war factories, starting a photography business and a camera store, clerking for garment companies, going into show business, touring America, doing commercials, going back to school. . . . It was a twentieth-century life. Born in 1918, died in 2000, she began to seem to me representative of millions of women who had passed through the same time period: the end of World War I, the Depression, the New Deal, World War II, the Korean War, the civil rights movement, Vietnam and the antiwar movement, gay rights, feminism. Her very discontent seemed emblematic of millions of other women's experiences, or so I have told myself, while working on this book, trying to quiet the carping voice that said: Who's going to care about your mother enough to want to read it?

I am well aware that if I had transformed this account into my own prose, it might have read more smoothly, more palatably. My mother could exasperate or get on a reader's nerves, just as she sometimes did on mine. But I opted for large sections of the transcribed tapes, more or less verbatim, because they graphically showed, to me at least, how one edges toward an insight and then backs away, how we rationalize or shift the blame onto others. I chose to include so much of her testimony verbatim because it seemed a more realistic presentation of the person she was, and the dynamic between us. (Realism, that old, disabused deity.) So yes, there is a scientific streak in me that is curious about the way people talk, and that would be inclined to diagram interactional patterns. The tapes also showed, in spite of the love and goodwill between us, how the wariness between a parent and a grown child might not overcome a certain impasse. The stalemate between us was unbreakable: we were too much alike. When I showed an earlier draft of this manuscript to someone, he was dismayed that there seemed to be no change in my views of my mother from my earlier self to my present one—no softening. This is true. I would have been happy to demonstrate some eureka, some redemptive insight that deepened or warmed my feelings, but in truth there was no *On Golden Pond* moment during her lifetime when we fell into each other's arms, and since she is gone I have not found it any easier to embrace her ghost. I was raised by a powerful woman, and the defenses I developed against her have not essentially altered, any more than have the admiration, gratitude, and fascination I feel for her.

I sometimes think that I was put on earth to understand my mother's pain and have not gotten very far in the process. I strived to empathize, but then her complaints would go on a little too long—no matter what she achieved, she was always lamenting that she had gotten "the shitty end of the stick," in her words—and I would pull back. As for understanding my mother's pleasure, that is equally problematic. A part of me equitably accepts that she did what she had to do, in pursuing amorous affairs and cheating on my father; who can blame her for wanting love, or sexual happiness, for that matter? But as her son, it rankled. I think it rankled in part because, as much as I didn't want my mother hovering over me, I was threatened growing up whenever her attention was taken away by other men, by another life outside the home. Dorothy Dinnerstein, in her feminist classic, *The Minotaur and the Mermaid,* posited that the root of men's misogyny was their never being able to forgive the mother for their humiliating dependency on her when they were infants and little children. It's entirely possible. Then again, the mistrust between men and women cuts both ways. My mother had a profound mistrust of men, including her sons, even as she craved them.

I have to admit I also wanted her voice so fully on the page as a record simply to honor her. "Attention must be paid!" and so forth. That line from *Death of a Salesman* has always struck me as a little foolish and blustery. *Why* must attention be paid? In truth, attention need not be paid, and rarely is, in the great scheme of things. It's understandable that a son might want to pay heed to his mother's tale, but that does not mean anyone else is obligated to care. Still, we writers feel a need to preserve everything. Where's the harm?